# Knitting

## —FOR—

# Peace

# Knitting
## —FOR—
# Peace

MAKE the WORLD a BETTER PLACE
ONE STITCH at a TIME

**BETTY CHRISTIANSEN**

PHOTOGRAPHS BY KIRIKO SHIROBAYASHI

STC CRAFT | A MELANIE FALICK BOOK      STEWART, TABORI & CHANG | NEW YORK

Published in 2006 by Stewart, Tabori & Chang
An imprint of Harry N. Abrams, Inc.

Versions of "Rebuilding Lives, Stitch by Stitch: Snow Cabin Goods," "Knitting a Safer World: Sheila's Shawls,"
and "Knitting Behind Bars: Prison Knitting" have appeared in *Interweave Knits* magazine.

Editor: Melanie Falick
Designer: goodesign
Production Manager: Jane Searle

Library of Congress Cataloging-in-Publication Data:
Christiansen, Betty.
  Knitting for peace : make the world a better place one stitch at a time/Betty Christiansen.
    p. cm.
  Includes index.
  ISBN-13: 978- 1-58479-533-9
  ISBN-10: 1-58479-533-6
  1. Knitting—Patterns. 2. Knitting—Social aspects. 3. Charity. I. Title.

TT820.C4957 2006
746.43'2—dc22

2006001296


The text of this book was composed in Clarendon and Neutra.

Printed and bound in China
10 9 8 7 6 5

**HNA**
**harry n. abrams, inc.**
a subsidiary of La Martinière Groupe
115 West 18th Street
New York, NY 10011
www.hnabooks.com

FOR ANDREW, WHO BRINGS ME PEACE

# Table of Contents

★ ★ ★ ★ ★ ★ ★ ★ ★ ★ ★ ★ ★ ★ ★ ★ ★ ★ ★ ★ ★ ★ ★ ★ ★ ★ ★ ★ ★ ★ ★ ★ ★ ★ ★ ★ ★ ★ ★ ★

★ ★ ★ ★ ★ ★ ★ ★ ★ ★ ★ ★ ★ ★ ★ ★ ★ ★ ★ ★ ★ ★ ★ ★ ★ ★ ★ ★ ★ ★ ★ ★ ★ ★ ★ ★ ★ ★ ★ ★ ★ ★ ★ ★ ★

# Introduction

NOT SO MANY YEARS AGO, I BEGAN KNITTING FOR PEACE. I RESPONDED TO A FLYER I DISCOVERED ONE JANUARY AT A ST. PAUL YARN SHOP. The Minnesota Knitters Guild was collecting "Cardigans for Deserving Babies"—babies born at local hospitals who hadn't a stitch of warm clothing to wear home. Something about these thinly clad babies pierced my heart. I knew exactly what yarn to use, and, once home, I dug it out of my stash with a particular urgency. I remember picking out buttons—washable— that would contrast brightly with the blue yarn I used. I remember blocking the sweater and folding it just so, creating a sweet package deserving of the baby who'd receive it. I wondered about this baby and wished it well. I thought of the mother and what she might think of this anonymous gift. I wondered what would become of the child—and the sweater—over the years. Then I dropped it back off at the yarn store, my questions unanswered, but no matter.

Knitters have been doing this kind of work well before I discovered it for myself. They've long been gathering in yarn stores and guild meetings, calling the work they do "charity knitting," "community knitting," or "knitting for others." They knit whole afghans, piece by piece; they knit preemie caps to warm heads the size of oranges; they knit lap blankets and mittens and socks and hats. They knit for people in their hometowns and for people across the planet, and they do it selflessly and willingly. Throughout the generations, they have knit for soldiers and civilians in battles from the Revolutionary War to the recent conflicts in Iraq. They knit for countless reasons, but they all share one thing in common: a desire to knit the world into a better place, through handmade gifts of love and peace.

As a contributor to magazines like *Vogue Knitting*, *Family Circle Easy Knitting*, and *Interweave Knits*, I found myself frequently talking to and writing about knitters who were doing just that, and I discovered that knitting was helping people all over the world in amazing ways. Who knew, for instance, that knitting could be used as a therapeutic tool for inmates in prisons? Or that knitting could help heal the shattered lives of women survivors of the war in Bosnia? Or that ordinary people—say, a yarn store owner in Wisconsin, or a laid-off dotcommer in San Francisco, or two friends in Connecticut—could start national charity knitting movements? And how did that happen?

What were their stories? I wanted to know, and in celebration of what these people were doing— what knitting can do—I wanted to share them with you.

Sit down with any knitter, pull out your needles, and stories are soon to flow. And as I contacted the individuals and organizations featured in this book—some well-known to me and others found through labyrinthine Internet searches or serendipity—flow they did. I was surprised by the generosity of spirit I encountered with every phone call I made; every person featured here is passionate about her or his cause, and grateful for every single knitter who has contributed. Most of the charity organizations featured here began as one person's good idea, and were—and often still are—run from that person's dining-room table or spare bedroom, where knitted donations pile up despite the dismay of family members. It's this humble quality inherent in every organization featured here that impresses me most. Knitting for peace is not about credit or praise. There is no room for ego. It's about helping people, pure and simple.

I expected to be uplifted by what these people had to tell me. What I didn't expect was that my heart would be broken, many times over, by the hard realities of orphans in Russia, or children with AIDS in South Africa, or any number of the desperate situations American children are in when they receive a "Binky," or women when they receive a prayer shawl. I didn't expect to be left speechless on the phone when I learned the impact one knit item—a blanket, a shawl, a teddy bear—could have in the face of almost any tragedy. "It makes me want to knit for them all," I told someone during an interview. "But I can't. That's why I'm writing this book."

We knitters work a powerful magic when we knit for others. By doing so, as you will see in the pages that follow, we can build bridges between warring nations, help to heal deep wounds, offer a primal sort of comfort, and create peace—however small, and in whatever way that may be—for others and ourselves.

I hope you will be as inspired by these groups and as filled with hope as I have been while researching and writing this book. The groups featured here—and those who knit for them and so many others—create in me a new excitement for the future of humanity. We can, stitch by stitch, inch the world in a more positive direction. We do this by knitting for peace. ★

# Peace

—AND—

# War

# A History of Wartime Knitting

THERE WOULD SEEM, AT FIRST GLANCE, TO BE NOTHING PEACEFUL ABOUT KNITTING IN TIMES OF WAR. TO MANY, KNITTING TO SUPPORT THOSE FIGHTING IN WAR MAY SEEM AS THOUGH IT SUPPORTS THE WAR ITSELF. BUT PEACE IS NOT A COMMODITY EXCLUSIVE TO PACIFISTS. ANYONE IN A DIFFICULT SITUATION—FROM WAR REFUGEES TO SOLDIERS ON BATTLEFRONTS—DESERVES SOME MEASURE OF PERSONAL PEACE. THAT IS WHAT HAS INSPIRED KNITTERS THROUGHOUT HISTORY TO KNIT FOR THEM ALL, ESPECIALLY DURING THE MOST DEVASTATING AND DEMORALIZING TIMES. ☮ You don't have to embrace war to knit for warriors, as Jeanne Dykstra, who organizes an effort to knit for troops stationed in Iraq, points out. "These soldiers are America's children," she states, echoing the words of people who have been carrying on a tradition of "knitting for

Sammy," "knitting their bit," or "knitting for the boys" (and girls) that has lasted more than two hundred years.

America was founded in an act of noncompliance, and it's no surprise that colonial knitters stitched in that spirit as well. Britain's tight restrictions on its colonies led American colonists to dig in their heels. Spinning, weaving, knitting, and sewing, formerly seen as domestic roles of the "weaker sex," became a new way to assert American independence. Home production of clothing became a protest; spinning bees and knitting circles became resistance movements.

When the Revolutionary War began, women were urged to "cast their mite into the public good," to assist the government in clothing its army, and they did not disappoint. From Virginia to New

Jersey, they furiously knit socks and sewed shirts for the soldiers—in addition to those they made for their own (usually sizeable) families. Others used their knitting to forward the war effort in more subversive ways. "Old Mom Rinker," a knitter near Philadelphia, passed on tidbits of British military information garnered from eavesdropping tavern keepers. In a way only a knitter could conceive of, she embedded notes to General Washington in balls of yarn, went to a cliff outside of town, and perched there with her knitting, the picture of innocence. When the general's troops passed along the path below, she would nudge a ball of yarn over the cliff edge, landing it at their feet. One of the troops would just as innocently pick it up, and the message would be hastened to General Washington.

Farm women living near Valley Forge, Pennsylvania, during the harsh and dispiriting winter of 1776 not only hand-knit but hand-delivered their goods, riding to the battlefront with saddlebags stuffed with hundreds of shirts, breeches, and socks.

Even Martha Washington knit for the war effort. An incessant knitter who often lived near the battlefront herself with her husband, she organized a war knitting group among officers' wives.

Almost a century later, during the Civil War, the pleas for knitted things—especially socks—came directly from the soldiers. Personal appeals, sent to mothers and sisters and wives in battlefield letters from soldiers with frostbitten feet and tattered boots, heightened the knitters' sense of urgency. With no government bidding, women automatically organized themselves to roll bandages, collect donations, and knit.

Knitters in the North were particularly efficient at organizing knitting and sewing circles, having long gathered for such domestic pursuits in church societies and social gatherings. They began knitting for young men from their own region, but the desire to knit in the spirit of Union solidarity—for any Union soldier on the battlefield—soon became apparent. In 1861, community leaders from across the North established the United States Sanitary Commission, a predecessor of the Red Cross that organized the charitable efforts of Northern women and streamlined the distribution of items to the Union soldiers. Together, women churned out gloves, mufflers, blankets, and a veritable flood of socks—all stamped "U.S. Sanitary Commission"—freely given to anonymous soldiers and often accompanied by a note of encouragement.

In the South, women faced more organizational obstacles—greater distances between their homes, few established sewing and knitting circles, scarce materials, and a prevailing belief in women's helplessness. But they cared for their soldiers as much as any woman in the North, and when the need arose, they knit just as determinedly. As in the North, Southern women knit first for their own sons and husbands, then the collective Confederate need. With battles occurring literally in their backyards, many women stuffed their pockets with socks and delivered them to soldiers themselves. Plantation houses were set up as knitting and sewing centers. War knitting bees offered camaraderie as well as a release for the knitters' fear and worry.

Everyone, it seems, in the North and South alike was enlisted to knit: expert older women, young belles, General Lee's wife, slaves, children, even convalescent soldiers. All efforts were welcomed. Whether a soldier was on the winning or losing side, whether he lived or died, his feet were warmed and, at least for a time, his spirits lifted.

A new generation of wartime knitting began in 1914, when Germany invaded Belgium and northern France, signaling the beginning of World War I. The Red Cross recruited knitters nationwide to clothe and comfort Allied soldiers, European civilians, and, eventually, U.S. troops. This effort was formalized in 1916; known as the Production Corps, it included knitting, sewing, and bandage-making. "Women at home during the war wanted to do something," says Thomas Goehner of the Red Cross

Museum, "and giving a part of themselves through knitting was a way they could contribute."

With headquarters in Washington, D.C., and chapters located nationwide, the Red Cross Production Corps was an efficient organization, able to quickly communicate specific knitting needs and distribute regulation yarns, patterns, and needles to knitters all over the world. Knitters were recruited through advertisements in local newspapers and the *Red Cross Magazine*, and knitting was promoted at bond rallies, war parades, and Red Cross meetings. Patterns were published by the Red Cross and other relief organizations, yarn manufacturers, needlework magazines, and even the *New York Times*. The Red Cross set quotas for each chapter and received handknit items by the millions, packed for immediate shipment to France. Between 1917 and 1919, when the war ended, more than 8 million Red Cross chapter members produced more

> **" If we have no peace, it is because we have forgotten that we belong to each other. "**
>
> MOTHER TERESA

★ ★ ★ ★ ★ ★ ★ ★ ★ ★ ★ ★ ★

During World War II, adherence to the regulation Red Cross patterns, which complied with military specifications, was of utmost importance. Even the colors had to satisfy military needs—olive drab for the Army, navy blue for the Navy. Into each item was sewn a label that read, "Gift of the American People thru the American Red Cross."

★ ★ ★ ★ ★ ★ ★ ★ ★ ★ ★ ★ ★

than 370 million relief articles for the Allied forces and civilians in Europe (though no records were kept of exactly how many of those were hand-knit).

But the knitting effort extended beyond the scope of the Red Cross. John D. Rockefeller opened his Fifth Avenue mansion in New York City to accommodate busy knitters, and the Navy League sponsored a three-day knitting bee in Central Park in 1918. Despite the withering heat, the bee yielded hundreds of woolen knit goods. Huskier sorts— firefighters, police officers, and even Governor Hunt of Arizona— took up their knitting for "Sammy," generating great publicity for the knitting cause. President Wilson allowed a flock of sheep to graze on the White House lawn; their shorn wool eventually sold for $1,000 a pound at a Red Cross auction.

Some critics suggested that all this knitting was a waste of time, energy, and resources, arguing that the items provided

were more "comforts" than "necessities." But soldiers in foxholes would probably have argued otherwise, and knitters certainly did. Their fingers flew throughout the war and well into its aftermath, when the Red Cross urged them to keep knitting garments for war refugees and hospitalized soldiers. In 1925, actress Mary Pickford—perhaps the first celebrity knitter—knit between scenes of her latest photoplay in support of ongoing Red Cross efforts.

When World War II began in 1939, knitters instinctively reached for their needles and, spurred on by such role models as Eleanor Roosevelt, began knitting once again "for the boys." They started by "knittin' for Britain" through the Red Cross Production Corps and Bundles for Britain, then for their own soldiers when the United States entered the war. Between 1939 and 1946, these knitters made an astonishing number of items—about 65 million, all told— for U.S. troops, Allies, and civilians.

For soldiers in trenches and on ships, only wool yarn would do, and it was supplied to the Red Cross by yarn companies such as Bear Brand and Bucilla. So much wool was consumed for the war effort that wool shortages occasionally stilled knitters' fingers until a new supply was acquired. Once received, garments were scrupulously inspected. Often-times, poorly knit items were ripped out by Production Corps sticklers and reknit or returned to the knitter. Even the packaging of knit items was strictly prescribed by Production Corps officials; the post-knitting instructions for the Red Cross-approved muffler direct knitters to fold it in half five times, then tie securely in pack-ages of five.

The knitting efforts of World War II were colored by a new generation and a new era. More celebrities were knitting, ditties about knitting were playing on the radio, and college coeds were taking up knitting in droves. Department stores and fashion magazines touted the benefits of wartime knitting, realizing the impact this could have on their sales. Knitters only knit harder, with ever-altruistic intentions. They may not have been working in munitions factories, but they were helping.

Even after World War II ended, knitters of the Red Cross Production Corps stayed active for many years, knitting for veterans and refugees. When the Korean War began in 1950, relief efforts toward Korean people—especially orphaned children—spurred knitters affiliated with organiza-tions like Church World Service to knit once more. But as time went on, military needs and women's roles changed, and with them, the necessity of knitting for soldiers. The Red Cross phased out its Production Corps in the 1960s, and little evidence exists of knitting either for troops or refugees during the Vietnam War.

Today, knitting for troops stationed abroad—some actively involved in war—is once again a high priority for many knitters. Groups like The Ships Project, Operation Toasty Toes, and others coordinate nationwide knitting efforts to supply soldiers with warm slippers, hats, and other comfort items (see page 19) Knitting guilds, after-school programs, and other small, localized knitting groups support units in which community members and loved ones are stationed. All fulfill an important role: bringing a bit of peace and joy to soldiers in some of the least peaceful places on earth. ★

To learn more about the subject of wartime knitting or the role of knitting in American culture generally, seek out a copy of the wonderful book *No Idle Hands: The Social History of American Knitting*, from which much of the information in this chapter was drawn. Written by Anne Macdonald, it is an informative and charming look at the history of the craft in America.

# Red Cross Knitters Remember

The Red Cross is nearly synonymous with wartime knitting. Ask knitters of a certain age about it, and you'll find many of them have stories of knitting furiously in movie theaters, in classes, and at Red Cross meetings for the "boys" stationed overseas. They knit for sons, for husbands, for sweethearts, and for no particular soldier at all. Knitting became their patriotic duty, the one thing they could do to honor those defending the United States.

For some women, like Karel Lea Biggs of Clarksville, Tennessee, knitting for soldiers was a tradition passed down through generations. "My grandmother taught me to knit," Karel says. "She told me her grandmother, the daughter of a Civil War Union general, taught her during World War I, when she was about nine. She learned by knitting olive green squares, which were sewn together to make blankets that were sent to the soldiers in Europe."

Other knitters were taught as children in schools or as Junior Red Cross members. "I learned to knit in third grade," says World War II knitter Shirley Robb of Decatur, Georgia, "when all the girls were taught to knit. As an eleven-year-old Girl Scout, I knitted bandages for the Red Cross: size 30 crochet thread, size 1 double-pointed needles, thirty stitches, garter stitch. Endless knitting." Helping the Red Cross in this way made for a new generation of proud—if sometimes bored—wartime stitchers.

Maria Kaiser of Raleigh, North Carolina, remembers her grandmother knitting scarves and helmet liners for troops in World War II. "She was a constant knitter," Maria says. "I remember her knitting in the dark of a movie theater. My mother knitted one scarf," she adds. "But that was her only knitting venture, and she said she felt sorry for the soldier who received it."

Scarves, helmet liners, hats, socks, gloves, mittens, vests, and sweaters—all were needed and abundantly knit by Red Cross volunteers. "I was sixteen years old when I knit long stockings for the Red Cross," remembers World War II knitter Alice Tabak of Brooklyn, New York, who, at age eighty-one, has long lost track of how many pairs she knit. "They gave me off-white woolen yarn and needles. It felt so good to know I was doing such a useful project."

---

**KNITTING FOR THE RED CROSS**
For more information on the Red Cross knitting tradition, visit www.redcross.org/museum/history/productioncorps.asp and www.redcross.org/article/0,1072,0_332_2774,00.html.

To try your hand at some Red Cross regulation knits from World Wars I and II, visit www.redcross.org/museum/exhibits/knits.asp.

Californian Janet Shott recalls knitting six-inch squares for soldiers' blankets every Friday afternoon at school when she was in fourth grade. "And if you were lucky enough to be selected," she adds, "you would be let into school early to sit at the 'Knit for the Boys' table," where schoolchildren rallied their peers to pick up needles, recruiting them as they walked in the door every morning. "That was our way to participate," she says. "We were so proud."

SENDING PEACE TO WAR ZONES
## The Ships Project

Ellen Harpin's Ships Project, a nationwide knitting-for-troops endeavor, stemmed from one short letter—a message "to any sailor" she penned shortly after September 11, 2001. The letter found its way to a soldier stationed on the USS *Bataan* at that time, a woman named Gloria. Noting that Ellen was a knitter, the sailor casually suggested that she should knit a pair of slippers for her. Ellen did not disappoint.

"After Gloria received the slippers, she wrote back and said her friends wanted them too. She asked for sixty more pairs," Ellen laughs. She sent out a request for help to her online knitting group, and answers—and slippers—came trickling in. By December, she had started her own Internet knitting list, originally called the Bataan Project, and hundreds of knitters signed on. Ellen's project, now known as The Ships Project, has steadily grown to more than a thousand knitters, and the total of knit items sent exceeds 175,000. These items have been sent to soldiers on ships and bases in locations like Iraq, Afghanistan, Kuwait, Qatar, and Uzbekistan.

Since her project began, Ellen has built solid relationships with military personnel. These connections allow her slippers and other knitted goods to reach soldiers whose movements are classified, like those on submarines and in special operations. "It was a

★ ★ ★ ★ ★ ★ ★ ★ ★ ★ ★ ★

**WHAT THEY NEED**

• The most-needed knitted items for troops are hats and slippers. The hats usually need to fit under helmets, so they should be close-fitting, not too bulky, and without cuffs or brims. Slippers need to be sized for adult men and women.

• While any color will do for most items, masculine colors are preferred (most of the troops are male). Please avoid pastels. Slippers can be knit in any color, as can hats bound for soldiers stationed on ships. Hats for ground troops should be knit in shades of brown, tan, gray, black, or desert camouflage (not the green-shaded jungle camouflage).

• While wool provides the most warmth, acrylic yarns are also acceptable, and wool/acrylic blends work well. If you are using a wool that is not machine-washable, tag the item "hand-wash only."

★ ★ ★ ★ ★ ★ ★ ★ ★ ★ ★ ★

hard sell originally," she says about clearing some soldiers' requests. "Now the units come to us. We've never said no; we've never let them down." Her efforts have been recognized not only by the soldiers, but also by the industry. She was named Knitter of the Year in 2005 by *Knitter's* magazine and Lion Brand Yarn Company.

Ellen insists that anyone can knit for soldiers, regardless of their views on war. All that matters is that American men and women stationed overseas—many of whom never receive anything from home—are shown that someone stateside, even someone they've never met, is thinking of them. "I got a letter from one soldier who said that when we sent him his slippers"—custom-knit in a size 16— "we ruined his suicide plans."

As with knitting-for-troops efforts throughout history, this one encompasses knitters from all walks of life, all with different talents to contribute. "We have a knitter who's five, and we had one who was 101," says Ellen of her Ships Project participants. "Some of our knitters are men. They all can relate," she continues. "Everybody knows somebody over there."

CONSTRUCTIVE REVOLUTION
## The Revolutionary Knitting Circle

Grant Neufeld is a calm, soft-spoken man with an understated sense of humor, maybe not the type of person one would associate with the word *revolution*. And his organization, the Revolutionary Knitting Circle (RKC), is similar—revealing that knitting and revolutions are in fact related, and that, together, they can produce very constructive results.

Grant, an activist in Calgary, Alberta, began RKC in 2000 to protest globalization during the World Petroleum Conference held there. "A story had emerged about a peace group in Europe that spent a day knitting at a major intersection well traveled by military vehicles," he says. "By the end of the day, they had completed a massive net that they stretched across the intersection, effectively shutting it down." Though Grant was never able to verify that story, it inspired him nonetheless. "It was such a strong image," he says, "yet very peaceful." RKC was organized in that spirit—that a serene and thoroughly nonviolent act, like knitting, could be used to make a statement for social justice and for peace.

The group made another prominent appearance at the Group of Eight (G8) economic summit in 2002, also held in Calgary, where about 1,000 protesters took to the streets. In sharp contrast to the violent demonstrations that took place at the G8 meeting in Genoa, Italy, the year before, Grant and about eighty other revolutionary knitters staged a knit-in, calmly knitting and politely interacting with passersby curious about what they were stitching and why. "The RKC connects with people in a way that protests, marches, and sit-ins don't," he says. "It creates a setting of nonhostility, and the knitters are not ignored. People will come up and ask what I'm knitting. It's usually something protest-related"—say, a peace armband or a square for a peace banner—"and it leads to a conversation." Knitting has an effect on more traditional activists as well. "Having knitting present at an activist meeting, where things can get pretty heated, makes the space calmer," he says. "That's a nice side effect."

Grant himself was not a knitter until he started the RKC, which he describes as a "loosely knit" group with a following that extends across Canada, the United States, and Europe. "We have no official chapters," he says. "It has a life of its own. People are using it to forward their own causes in their own communities." He does, however, encourage organizers to engage a diverse range of participants and to keep knitting at the forefront. "We encourage skill sharing," he says. "We teach others to knit." That includes passersby whose interest has been piqued.

The group's goals consist of "mainly simple stuff," Grant says, "like eradicating the authoritarian corporatist state." But at its core is a philosophy of self-sufficiency that has made knitting and other handcrafts tools for noncompliance that have been employed for

KNITTING FOR THE RKC
For more information on the Revolutionary Knitting Circle, including patterns for peace armbands and banners, contact:

Revolutionary Knitting Circle
P.O. Box 21022
665 Eighth Street SW
Calgary, Alberta
Canada T2P 4H5
www.knitting.activist.ca
knitting@activist.ca

> "
> **Peace cannot be attained through violence, it can only be attained through understanding.**
> "
>
> RALPH WALDO EMERSON

centuries (consider Gandhi spinning fiber in solidarity with Indian hand-spinners forced into unemployment by mechanized mills, or the founding mothers of the United States spinning and knitting to end dependence on British materials). "We hold that all communities should have the means necessary to meet every essential need of their own people," the RKC manifesto declares. "By sharing in the skills and resources of our communities, we shall become free to cast off dependencies on global trade for our subsistence."

Critics have called the RKC hooligans bent on destruction, even terrorists. But the presence of knitting makes such claims seem downright silly. "I don't want to destroy lives," says Grant. "I want to create something better. When we are engaged in knitting, we are doing that in a very concrete way. We are creating community and local independence, which, in this corporate society, is a truly revolutionary act."

## Wednesdays at Elegant Stitches

In Jeanne Dykstra's yarn shop, Elegant Stitches, in Miami, Florida, there's a wall covered with photos and letters from soldiers stationed in Iraq and Afghanistan. The letters express appreciation to the women who gather at the store every Wednesday to knit and sew for them. "These soldiers are now like adopted friends and children," Jeanne says of the nine units to whom she sends everything from knitted slippers and hats to drink mixes, bedsheets, and coffee makers.

"I started knitting for a young friend of mine whose unit was sent to Iraq," she says. "In the summer, it's about 120 degrees there, but in October, the temperatures plummet. These guys were sleeping in a bombed-out palace with marble floors and no heat," she says. "So we started knitting them hats and socks and slippers. The soldiers call us fairy godmothers."

American soldiers in Iraq, especially those actively engaged in war, need all the support knitters can give. "All my units are located in danger zones," Jeanne says. "Day-to-day life is hell. Imagine patrolling all day, wearing fifty to seventy pounds of gear, and it's 115 degrees. Your camp is being mortared regularly. When you get home, you're exhausted

**LEARN MORE**
For more opportunities to knit for troops, contact:

Elegant Stitches
8841 SW 132 Street
Miami, FL 33176
(305) 232-4005
www.elegant-stitches.com

Operation Home Front
www.operationhomefront.org/community/knitters.shtml
operationhomefront@operationhomefront.org

Operation Toasty Toes
www.operationtoastytoes8.gobot.com
opertt8@yahoo.com

and hot—but there's a box waiting for you. And you forget everything else. That's why we do this. Our children—America's children—are over there," she adds, "and they need us."

BIG LOSSES, SMALL SWEATERS
## Red Sweaters

Two years after the conflict in Iraq began, knitter Nina Rosenberg conceived of a new way to knit in response to war. She set out to create an art installation of tiny, handknit red sweaters—one to represent each American soldier who died in Iraq—connected in a chain and displayed on a tree in front of her San Francisco home. "I wanted to use my knitting skills for something war-related," says Nina, "but I have no direct tie to anyone fighting over there. I felt very disassociated with the war, and I knew other people did too. I wanted to do something that would touch others who felt as disassociated as I did."

In the course of one sleepless night, she came up with a solution: Recruit knitters to make small red sweaters—sized to fit G.I. Joe dolls, not coincidentally—that could be displayed publicly as a visual reminder of the American lives lost in Iraq. She chose sweaters because they're representative of the human form, and red for the color of blood. "At first, I wanted to represent *all* lives lost, Iraqi and American," she says, but the number of sweaters required was overwhelming. She chose to focus on the American death toll, which, at the time she began her project, totaled around 1,500.

Reaching out to knitters on "as many Internet groups as I could find," Nina spread word of her project, posted instructions on her website, and watched the sweaters come in. "People knit these sweaters for their own reasons," she says, careful to emphasize that the project itself is not intended to be a war protest, nor a memorial, but a tool for raising awareness and inspiring

**LEARN MORE ABOUT RED SWEATERS**
For information on participating in or viewing the Red Sweaters installation, visit www.red sweaters.org.

thought and discussion about the war. "Some do knit because they're against the war. About half knit to remember the soldiers. Others knit to honor someone they have lost," she adds. "All sides are represented."

The installation will continue to change as sweaters are added to reflect the rising death toll. "I'll leave it up until it seems right to take it down," she says, "when the war is over or the neighbors complain." Until then, she hopes it will stimulate viewers to think about the war and how it affects them in ways they have not yet considered. It's already doing that among the participating knitters. "Some of my knitters are women in their seventies who hadn't knit for twenty or thirty years," says Nina. "But they felt they had to pick up their needles for this."

# Knitting for Peace Messenger Bag

WAGE PEACE BY CARRYING YOUR KNITTING AROUND IN THIS FELTED MESSENGER BAG. STURDY AND GOOD-SIZED—IT'S LARGE ENOUGH TO ACCOMMODATE PLENTY OF YARN AND ANY LENGTH OF NEEDLE—IT CLOSES WITH A FLAP EMBLAZONED WITH THE KNITTING FOR PEACE LOGO.

THE BAG IS SIMPLE TO KNIT: THE BASE IS A GARTER-STITCH RECTANGLE, AND STITCHES ARE PICKED UP ALONG ALL FOUR EDGES OF IT TO FORM THE BODY, ALL WORKED IN THE ROUND. STITCHES ARE THEN DIVIDED FOR THE FLAP AND THE STRAPS, WORKED BACK AND FORTH.

FINISHED MEASUREMENTS
20" wide, 20½" tall, and 5" deep before felting; 14" wide, 12" tall, and 3½" deep after felting

YARN: Approximately 800 yards heavy worsted-weight yarn (must be wool or other feltable animal fiber; do not use superwash wool or wool/acrylic blends)

Sample shown in Cascade Yarns Pastaza (50% llama/50% wool)

NEEDLES: One 24" circular needle (circ) size US 10½ (6.5 mm)
Change needle size if necessary to obtain correct gauge.

NOTIONS: Yarn needle, stitch markers, stitch holders, plus for logo (optional) computer with scanning capabilities, printer, T-shirt transfer paper (sold at craft and stationery stores), iron, muslin or other light-colored fabric slightly larger than logo, sewing needle, and thread.

GAUGE: 12 sts = 4" (10 cm) in Stockinette stitch (St st) before felting (row gauge is not crucial)

## Base
CO 60 sts.
Begin in Garter st (knit every row); work 34 rows even.

## Body
Work 60 sts, place marker (pm), pick up and knit 17 sts on short side of base (1 st in each garter ridge), pm, 60 sts along the next long side of base (1 st in each st), pm, 17 sts along remaining short side of base, pm (preferably a different color

marker than the rest, as this one will mark the beginning of your rnd). Join for working in the rnd—154 sts.

Rnd 1: K60, sl 1 st, k15, sl 1 st, k60, sl 1 st, k15, sl 1 st.
Rnd 2: Knit.
Repeat Rnds 1 and 2 until sides of bag measure 20½", ending at beginning of round.
Divide sts for strap and flap as follows: BO next 60 sts (for top front opening of bag), k17 sts and place on holder (for left side of strap), k60 sts (for flap) and leave on needle, place remaining 17 sts (right side of strap) on holder.

## Flap
With 60 sts remaining on needle, work back and forth as follows:
Row 1 (RS): Knit.
Row 2 (WS): K1, purl to last st, k1.
Repeat Rows 1 and 2 until flap measures 19" from beginning, ending with a RS row.
Change to Garter st; work 4 rows.
BO all sts.

## Strap

Place one set of strap sts on needle (17 sts). Work back and forth as follows:
Row 1 (RS): Knit.
Row 2 (WS): K1, purl to last st, k1.
Repeat Rows 1 and 2 until strap measures 22" from beginning. Place sts on holder. Repeat the above steps for the second half of strap. Using the Kitchener st (page 126), graft the sts together at top of strap.

## Felting

Using yarn needle, weave in all loose ends. Place completed bag in a washing machine partially filled with hot water and a very small amount of detergent. Let it agitate for an entire cycle, checking every 10 minutes or so, and stopping when bag reaches desired dimensions (depending on the yarn used, this may take more than one cycle). When felting is complete, rinse bag in cold water and spin out excess water using the machine's spin cycle. Remove and shape as necessary, pulling and tugging the flap especially to achieve an even, square shape. Place a large shoebox or similarly shaped box inside the bag (to help shape it) and air dry.

## Add Logo

Scan the Knitting for Peace logo in the color of your choice at the back of the book. Following the instructions included with the T-shirt transfer paper, print the logo on the transfer paper. As evenly and neatly as possible, cut out the logo. Following the instructions included with the paper, iron the logo onto the fabric. If you want a clean (not frayed) edge around the logo, fold the edges of the fabric under, then sew the patch to your bag. If you like a frayed edge, cut away about 1/8" of fabric around the edges of the fabric, then sew the patch onto the bag. ★

Chapter
Two

# Peace
## —ON—
# Earth

# Peace Fleece

AT THE PEACE FLEECE FARM, SNUG-GLED IN THE FOOTHILLS OF THE WHITE MOUNTAINS IN WESTERN MAINE, PETER HAGERTY IS UP BEFORE DAWN. LIKE MANY FARMERS IN THIS PART OF MAINE, HE BEGINS THE DAY BY LIGHTING FIRES IN WOOD-BURNING STOVES IN THE FARMHOUSE AND BARN. HE FEEDS HIS ANIMALS—THE DRAFT HORSES HE STILL USES TO WORK THE FIELDS, AND THE SHEEP. BUT BEFORE HE ENGAGES IN THESE RATHER TYPICAL FARM DUTIES, HE CHECKS HIS E-MAIL FOR NEWS FROM HIS BUSINESS PARTNERS—IN RUSSIA. ☮ Since 1985, Peter and his wife, Marty Tracy, have been working closely with farmers in the former Soviet Union, buying wool and forming relationships in the hope that, through trade and a mutual wish for harmony by ordinary citizens on both sides of the Cold War, a sort of grassroots peace could be fostered. They hoped to accomplish this through the making of a humble product: a yarn called Peace Fleece, spun from the wool of U.S. and Soviet sheep.

What Peace Fleece has done in the years since—bringing together farmers and artisans in the United States, Russia, Eastern Europe, and the Middle East—might be called a "wool revolution," quiet and gentle but effective nonetheless.

"It's a funky little operation," Marty says of Peace Fleece, whose offices are situated in a three-story hay barn. "But it's a thriving, humming thing." Twenty years after it began, and well after the Soviet Union's collapse, Peace Fleece is scurrying to keep up with demand for its thick, richly colored Russian-American yarn. The Peace Fleece farm itself is a place where hope and healing seem as abundant as the hay in the fields or the sheep in the pasture. Local at-risk kids spend time here, finding therapy in caring for the horses. Peter himself sought healing when he and Marty moved here in 1973, shortly after his return from the Vietnam War. But the ultimate purpose of Peace Fleece has been to cure a particular and overwhelming hopelessness shared by many Americans—and Soviets—at the height of the Cold War.

"When we first started Peace Fleece in 1985," says Peter, "I was very convinced we were going to die in a nuclear war. I needed to find a way out of a depression I couldn't shake."

"We were both very, very upset," adds Marty. "We felt like we had to do something, we had to act. It was the only thing that seemed to calm us down."

"When you really get worried about this kind of stuff," Peter continues, "I've learned that if you can just get on the phone and talk to the person on the other side of the conflict, even though you may not totally resolve the problem, just starting the resolution can make you feel so much better." With the belief that agriculture can be a medium that brings people together, Peter came up with the idea of finding a Soviet farmer who, like him, grew wool. "We thought we'd see if we couldn't get Soviet and American farmers together," he says, "to make a product called Peace Fleece."

Peter is a natural-born storyteller and, in his words, the story of how Peace Fleece came to be takes on an almost legendary quality. "I was forty-one when I first went to Russia," he says, "and not at a good point in my life. I had been pretty angry coming back from Vietnam, and I had moved to the farm pretty angry, and I knew what I was against, but I didn't know what I was for." In the spring of 1985, he boarded a plane to Moscow and began to find out.

"I didn't speak any Russian at all, and I didn't know anyone," he continues, "but I had this idea of meeting a Russian farmer. I walked out of my hotel on a Friday morning and looked around. Across Red Square, there was a hotel with a name I could read: the Hotel Nationale. I walked in and started wandering aimlessly." When he got to the fourth floor, he found a door with a brass plaque bearing the name and address of a New York company. He tapped on the door, and it was answered by a woman who looked at him and declared, "I danced with you in the eleventh grade."

As it happens, this acquaintance, miraculously resurfacing in this foreign place, was exactly the person Peter needed. The woman and her husband, agents for a small American company well known and respected in Russia, quickly put him in contact with a wool broker named Nikolai Emelianov, who agreed to sell Peace Fleece its first Soviet wool. In February of 1986, after a

> ❝
> **You must be the change you wish to see in the world.**
> ❞
>
> MAHATMA GANDHI

circuitous journey, this small bale of wool arrived at Boston Harbor—where the longshoremen promptly refused to off-load it because it was a communist product. The story hit the Associated Press, and Peace Fleece was instantly in the public eye. "The story of a small family farm in Maine doing trade with the Soviet Union was just too good to pass up," Peter says.

Marty adds another perspective: "I saw this tiny, crummy bale of wool," she says, "and I was thinking, 'We're going to start a business with this?'" But she abandoned her work as a potter and signed on fully nonetheless. She has been coordinating the business end of Peace Fleece ever since.

It may seem that a small company like Peace Fleece could not have had much impact on the Cold War, but consider that, at the time, it was part of a movement in which American and Soviet citizens reached out to each other to discover a mutual hope for peace that built important bridges between the two nations. Once,

while traveling in the farthest corners of the Soviet Union to meet with farmers, Peter discovered a group of Idahoans in an obscure Central Asian hotel. "They said, 'We just decided to meet the folks over here. We decided to sit down with them and have a meal, maybe go for a walk.' It was just that kind of citizen's diplomacy that clicked the destruction meter slightly away from total annihilation," says Peter.

"That's what's so wonderful about knitting," he continues. "All these knitters used to go with us to Russia, and they'd sit in the middle of a square, and they'd just start knitting. Russian women would sit down next to them, and *they'd* start knitting, and they'd hang out all afternoon, laughing. Nobody was translating. It transcended any kind of nationalistic or language limitation, and I think that's what really allowed us to survive that terribly difficult time."

Having moved past the Cold War, Peace Fleece expanded its reach into other countries in conflict. During the

Gulf War in 1991, Peter traveled to Israel in an effort to create something similar to Peace Fleece there, bringing together Israeli and Palestinian farmers through wool. The program didn't take off quite the way the Russian endeavor did, as the dangers of interacting with each other became too great for farmers on both sides. Still, the weaving yarn offered by Peace Fleece is spun from Israeli and Palestinian wool, and all the proceeds of a particular color of Peace Fleece yarn—Baghdad Blue—help support Neve Shalom/Wahat al-Salam, a village in Israel established jointly by peace-seeking Jews and Palestinian Arabs.

The personal relationships Peter and Marty formed with farmers, businesspeople, and exporters in Russia count as some of the most rewarding aspects of Peace Fleece. "Our Russian office is in the home of the woman who's been our director for the last eleven years," Peter says. "And in that time, we've gone through everything together. We've shared their grief over the loss of a child and the joy of their children getting married." Understanding their lives shed light on the chaos and despair in which the Russians live. Obstacles like crime and threats to personal safety often interfered with the business. "In the beginning," says Peter, "the degree of dysfunctionalism in Russia was unbelievable. Nothing worked. I finally understood why things wouldn't get done. If a partner had to choose between making a deadline and making sure his child got home from school without harm, he would err on the side of the child. You couldn't argue with their choices. But it's a very difficult way to run a business."

In the last five years or so, much of that has changed. A partnership with a freight forwarding company in Yaroslavl has ensured that importing and exporting happen smoothly and efficiently. And while Russian wool is more and more difficult to come by due to a resurgence in Russia's domestic wool market that keeps most of it within its borders, new sources are being found in Romania.

Marty, with her artist's eye, sees improvement in another way. "I went to Russia in 1990," she says, "and I was just in shock. The roads were torn apart, there were no flowers, and people looked miserable. But when I went back two years ago, it was obvious to me that the spirit was lifting. You can see the health of a country by the art," she says. "If people create beauty, then you know they're feeling beautiful on the inside, and a society is in good shape."

Beauty and healing are reflected in all the products Peace Fleece offers, whether it's wool from Eastern European countries regaining their footing after oppression, or wool from Middle Eastern countries currently at war, or cheerful knitting needles and buttons hand-painted by Russian artisans. These products all illustrate the different ways knitting and peace are inextricably entwined. "It's all part of a human healing process," Peter says of knitting. Marty, too, believes that when people work with their hands, they open themselves to inner solutions for peace. "If everyone is more peaceful themselves," she says, "they have more tolerance to accept others and work out their own relationships. The back-and-forth process of people trusting each other, being patient with each other, listening to each other, following through—that's peace to me." It's this relationship-building process, besides the simple act of knitting for another, that she hopes true knitters-for-peace will engage in. ★

SUPPORTING PEACE FLEECE
For more information on Peace Fleece, or to purchase Peace Fleece yarn and other products, contact:

Peace Fleece
475 Porterfield Road
Porter, ME 04068
www.peacefleece.com
saw@peacefleece.com

31

# Peace Fleece Classic Wool Socks

## —DESIGNED BY PEG RICHARDS—

MADE FROM A HEAVY, DURABLE WOOL, THESE BASIC SOCKS ARE WARM AND COMFORTABLE. THE INSTRUCTIONS ARE EASY TO FOLLOW, EVEN FOR THOSE NEW TO SOCK KNITTING. ALTHOUGH THE PATTERN ONLY CALLS FOR ONE OR TWO COLORS, THESE SOCKS CAN ACTUALLY BE MADE IN AS MANY COLORS AS YOU WISH.

FINISHED MEASUREMENTS
Approximately 8 (8¾, 9½, 10½)" for adult Small (Medium, Large, Extra-Large)

YARN: Approximately 200 (200, 225, 250) yards worsted-weight yarn (MC) Approximately 50 (50, 75, 75) yards worsted-weight yarn (CC)

*Samples shown in Peace Fleece Worsted Weight (70% wool/30% mohair).*

NEEDLES: One set of four double-pointed needles (dpn) size US 5 (3.75 mm)
*Change needle size if necessary to obtain correct gauge.*

NOTIONS: Stitch marker, yarn needle

GAUGE: 20 sts and 30 rnds = 4" (10 cm) in Stockinette stitch (St st)

## Leg

With MC, CO 40 (44, 48, 52) sts. Distribute sts evenly on three needles. Join for working in the rnd, being careful not to twist sts; place marker for beginning of rnd. Work in k2, p2 ribbing until piece measures 2" from cast-on edge. Change to St st and CC (if using), and begin stripe pattern as follows: *Knit 3 rnds in CC, knit 3 rnds in MC. Repeat from * 5 times. Continue knitting in MC until piece measures 9" from cast-on edge, ending at beginning of rnd.

## Heel

Place the next 20 (22, 24, 26) sts on Needle 1 for Heel Flap. Distribute remaining sts evenly on remaining two needles. Using CC, work the sts on Needle 1 [Heel Flap] as follows:

Row 1: (RS) *Slip (sl) 1 st, k1, repeat from * across.
Row 2: (WS) Sl 1 st, purl across.

Repeat rows 1–2 until Heel Flap measures 2½ (2¾, 2¾, 3)". Place st marker at center of Heel Flap.

## Turn Heel

Row 1: (RS) Knit to 2 sts past center marker, k2tog, k1, turn.
Row 2 (WS): Purl to 2 sts past center marker, p2tog, p1, turn.
Row 3: Knit to 3 sts past center marker, k2tog, k 1, turn.
Row 4: Purl to 3 sts past center marker, p2tog, p1, turn.
Row 5: Knit to 4 sts past center marker, k2tog, k1, turn.
Row 6: Purl to 4 sts past center marker, p2tog, p 1, turn.
Row 7: Knit to 5 sts past center marker, k2tog, k1, turn.
Row 8: Purl to 5 sts past center marker, p2tog, p1, turn.

Continue decreasing in this manner until the last 2 sts at each end of needle have been knit or purled together, ending with a WS row—8 (10, 12, 14) sts remain.

## Heel Gusset

On RS, knit across Heel Flap. Change to MC and using same needle, pick up and knit 9 (10, 10, 11) sts along left side of Heel Flap (1 st in each slipped st); knit across Needles 2 and 3; using another needle pick up and knit 9 (10, 10, 11) sts along right side of Heel Flap (1 st in each slipped st); then knit across 17 (20, 22, 25) sts on Needle 1—46 (52, 56, 62) sts [26 (30, 32, 36) sts on Needle 1; 10 (11, 12, 13) sts on Needle 2; 10 (11, 12, 13) sts on Needle 3]. Continue knitting around, ending on Needle 3.

Begin Gusset decreases as follows: At the beginning of Needle 1, k1, skp, knit to last 3 sts on Needle 1, k2tog, k1. Knit even across Needles 2 and 3. Repeat decreases on heel needle in this manner until 20 (22, 24, 26) sts are left on Needle 1.

## Foot

Work even until foot measures 5¾ (6, 6½, 6¾)" from Heel Flap or 1 (1, 1½, 1¾)" less than desired length.

Change to CC, k 1 rnd even.

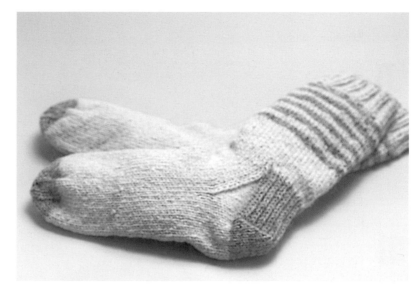

## Toe

Decrease Rnd: Begin on Needle 1, k1, skp, knit across needle to last 3 sts, k2tog, k1. On Needle 2, k1, skp, k to end of needle. On Needle 3, k across needle to last 3 sts, k2tog, k1.

Repeat this rnd until 8 sts remain. Graft sts using Kitchener Stitch (see page 126) or repeat the decrease rnd until 4 sts remain. Cut yarn, leaving a tail long enough to thread through remaining sts. Turn sock inside out, then draw tight, and fasten securely. Using yarn needle, weave in all loose ends. ★

# afghans for Afghans

THE AMERICAN FRIENDS SERVICE COMMITTEE OFFICE IN SAN FRANCISCO, CALIFORNIA, IS A NONDESCRIPT BUILDING ON THE FRINGE OF DOWNTOWN, NOT EXACTLY IN THE NICEST NEIGHBORHOOD, BUT A CENTER FROM WHICH GENEROSITY AND GOODWILL RADIATE. AT ITS BASEMENT LEVEL, THE ELEVATOR DOORS SLIDE OPEN TO REVEAL A DIMLY LIT, CEMENT-WALLED SPACE CLUTTERED WITH BOXES OF ALL SIZES AND SHAPES. ONE CORNER IN PARTICULAR IS STACKED WITH BOXES AND PACKAGES ADDRESSED TO AFGHANS FOR AFGHANS, ALL CONTAINING KNIT AND CROCHETED ITEMS DESIGNATED FOR FAMILIES IN AFGHANISTAN. ⊕ A substantial pile of donations has built up, and more are on their way. They're all earmarked for an afghans for Afghans campaign—a drive to collect 5,000 handknit wool hats, mittens, sweaters, vests,

socks, and of course, afghans. These donations will be sent to orphanages, clinics, and children's centers, arriving just in time for Afghanistan's notoriously harsh winter.

The volunteer packers gathered in this drab, gray place carry armfuls of these packages to a large table, and the fun begins. Quickly, the gloom of the basement is dispelled by a kaleidoscope of hats, sweaters, and blankets. The stillness is pierced by gasps of delight, and warmth exudes from the woolen items stacking up on all sides. "It's like opening presents," says volunteer Candace Key, and even though these packages aren't for anyone present, the sense of love and generosity with which they were given, and the sense of delight and wonder with which they are passed along, are tangible in the room.

Ann Rubin, the founder of afghans for Afghans, shares wholeheartedly in this wonder at the generosity of others. Particularly, she's pleased to report that the 5,000-item goal for this drive has been met. "I'm pretty sure that half of the items came in the last ten days before our due date," she says. At the last minute, as usual, knitters-for-peace all over the United States and Canada—and some from Europe and Australia—have come through. "People put so much time and creativity into them," she adds. Indicative of this are the notes tucked in among the knits: "I'm a novice knitter and this is the first hat I've ever knit!" writes one contributor. "I hope it's acceptable." Says another knitter of her boxful of items: "None of them are perfect, but they are full of good thoughts."

Ann first became intrigued by the Afghan people on a 1999

trip to Peshawar, Pakistan. From there, she traveled to the top of the Khyber Pass—the treacherous mountain passage leading into Afghanistan—where a large sign forbade foreigners from entering. At the time, she didn't fully understand why. "There were so many Afghan refugees in Peshawar," she remembers. "They'd come over by the truckful. In the bazaars and the markets, they were selling their personal possessions—beautiful textiles and material goods." It wasn't until September 11, 2001, and the subsequent U.S. presence in Afghanistan, that she learned the full impact of the Taliban rule and the plight of the long-oppressed Afghan people, now enduring a new war. At the time of the terrorist attacks, millions of Afghans were suffering from starvation, the country was in chaos, and winter was fast approaching.

Ann felt deeply compelled to help those people she'd met on her trip. "I want to send afghans to Afghans," she told someone in a play on words. (It's said that the word *afghan* was coined in the early 1800s because the patterns and colors of knit and crocheted blankets resembled those of rugs brought back from Afghanistan that were fashionable in Victorian households.) The name—and her determination—stuck.

"The AFSC and the local Afghan-American community were holding a blanket drive for Afghanistan," says Ann, adding that the San Francisco Bay Area is home to the largest population of Afghans in the United States. "I thought, let's *knit* blankets and send them along too." By the end of the year, she and her friends—technology professionals left unemployed by the market crash preceding September 11—had launched the afghans for Afghans website. Within a month, they had gathered a couple hundred handmade blankets, sent in from web-surfing knitters and crocheters all over North America, to add to the container bound for children

★ ★ ★ ★ ★ ★ ★ ★ ★ ★ ★ ★

Afghans for Afghans owes its beginnings to inspirations both historic and cutting-edge—the Red Cross knitting tradition and the Internet, respectively. "Many of us can remember our grandmas knitting for soldiers and refugees," says Ann, also inspired by her childhood reading of Louisa May Alcott's *Little Women*, in which the March sisters knit socks for Civil War soldiers as they waited for their father to come home from battle.

★ ★ ★ ★ ★ ★ ★ ★ ★ ★ ★

Perhaps one the most touching notes attached to a donation comes from Sgt. Claire Fron, a soldier serving in Iraq. "Enclosed is the baby blanket I knit," she writes. "Knitting has been a great stress reliever over here, so I decided to put it to a good use. I hope you find a good home for this blanket! It was made with love from one war-torn country to another."

★ ★ ★ ★ ★ ★ ★ ★ ★ ★ ★

and their families in Afghanistan. A second collection contained more handknit blankets as well as pieces of clothing—about 900 items in all. Since then, afghans for Afghans has held collection drives more or less quarterly and has delivered tens of thousands of items, knit by an incredibly wide spectrum of people.

"But I don't focus on numbers," says Ann. "I focus on the one-to-one connection. This is an expression of friendship and concern from U.S. and Canadian knitters. It's about the dignity of the individual," she adds, stressing that these are not merely handouts, that the recipients are not just destitute refugees. "The Afghans are a proud people with a rich history," she says. "Our point is to make something new and special for them, something more than warm clothes. Each item is a unique gift, given from one individual to another."

In celebration of the Afghans' own handcraft tradition, Ann offers knitting patterns inspired by Afghan designs for sale on the afghans for Afghans website. "The Afghans are good knitters," she says, noting that all their patterns are passed along orally, making documentation difficult. "There is a traditional sock pattern"—which can be purchased from the website—"that I swear is in their DNA." A portion of the proceeds from the sale of all such patterns, as well as from note cards picturing Afghan women spinning, benefits a women's literacy group in Afghanistan. Featuring this art, says Ann, gives knitters an appreciation of the Afghan people and their talents, but it also adds a reciprocal element. "That's what this is all about," says Candace, "sharing worlds with other people and bringing us closer together."

Creating a connection between knitters in the Western world and Afghans in need is one thing, but making the physical connection—getting boxes and boxes of handknits from a basement in San Francisco to a container on a plane to a truck traversing the mountainous roads of Afghanistan—is quite another. "Before the Taliban fell, we had to send the containers to Pakistan or Uzbekistan," Ann says. "Then once the Taliban were driven out, relief workers could bring the goods into Afghanistan." She adds that early afghans-for-Afghans knitters were a bit wary—how could they be certain these items would get to their intended recipients?

But thanks to a dedicated network made up of organizations like the AFSC, which offers a mailing address and storage space, and other reputable, experienced relief agencies that transport and distribute the goods in Afghanistan, the handknits arrive at their destinations safely. The photos on the afghans for Afghans website offer proof: children wearing brightly colored hats; veiled mothers clutching a baby in one arm and a parcel of knitwear in another. "This program works because of trust," says Ann. "Knitters trust that these items will get where they're supposed to."

Ever mindful of this, volunteer packers triple-tape each carton for extra durability. "We think of all the time that each of these knitters puts into these pieces," she says. "We want them to travel securely."

Still, the journey is tenuous, for afghans for Afghans as well as for the knits. Other world crises—tsunamis, hurricanes, the war in Iraq—have pushed Afghanistan far off the front page, making it difficult to keep the public's (and the knitters') attention. "We forget that Afghanistan is still really unstable," says Ann. "Life has improved since the fall of the Taliban, and reconstruction and development proceed, but deprivation, suffering, and violence still exist." For the relief workers who deliver the knitted goods and work with the Afghans directly, Afghanistan is still a very dangerous place to be. And while afghans for Afghans continues to meet its goals for most drives, Ann admits that it takes more work than ever to keep that flow constant, to keep word going out about the ongoing

need. "But we're not going to abandon Afghanistan," she says. "We're going to keep this program going to prove that point."

Her work is paying off—response to the project is still impressive. "People include notes to send along, and it's great for us to see their sentiment," says Candace. "And I always hope that the Afghans know that this came from a stranger who wishes them

well, who wishes them warmth, and health, and freedom, and security. I'm sure they can't read all that into these items. But if they just read a little of it, then a connection's been made, and that's why we do it." ★

### KNITTING FOR AFGHANS FOR AFGHANS

• Check the afghans for Afghans website, www.afghansforAfghans. org, frequently for information on the most recent program details, due dates, items needed, and shipping addresses. You can also e-mail afghans4Afghans@aol.com.

• While specific needs vary, the items most needed in Afghanistan are blankets, sweaters, vests, hats, socks, and mittens. Scarves and stuffed toys should not be sent.

• Items should be knit or crocheted with wool or wool-rich blends, which offer the most warmth.

Acrylic blankets are acceptable, but garments knit in acrylics and cottons will be donated to local charities instead.

• Please do not add representational images, such as faces, animals, or cartoon characters, to your knit pieces. (This restriction stems from a Muslim tradition that forbids the creation of a likeness of Allah.) Out of respect for the Afghans' culture, please avoid religious or national symbols as well.

• Use white and other light colors sparingly, as they are difficult to keep clean. Do, however, use green when possible—it's the beloved color of Islam.

# afghans for Afghans Child's Vest

## —DESIGNED BY SUSAN WILLS—

THIS VEST IS CLEVERLY KNIT FROM SIDE TO SIDE IN ONE PIECE TO CREATE VERTICAL STRIPES ON THE FRONT. IF WORKING A SOLID-COLORED VEST, IGNORE THE STRIPE INSTRUCTIONS AND BE SURE TO PLACE MARKERS WHERE INDICATED TO DISTINGUISH FRONT FROM BACK.

FINISHED MEASUREMENTS
22 (25, 28, 32)" chest
12½ (14½, 17½, 20)" length

YARN: Approximately 220 (280, 400, 600) yards worsted-weight yarn (MC), preferably wool
Small amounts worsted-weight yarn in at least two contrasting colors (A and B)

*Samples shown in Classic Elite Yarns Renaissance (100% wool)*

NEEDLES: One pair straight needles size US 7 (4.5 mm)
*Change needle size if necessary to obtain correct gauge.*

NOTIONS: Yarn needle, stitch markers, crochet hook size G/7 (4.5 mm), 4 buttons

GAUGE: 20 sts and 32 rows = 4" (10 cm) in Stockinette stitch (St st)

STRIPE PATTERN: Using colors as desired, alternate 4 rows of color A, 2 rows of color B in St st. Always begin new color at beginning of WS row. Weave in ends as you go or tie ends into square knots and trim. (The crochet edge will cover the knots.)

## Right Front

Using MC, CO 41 (49, 59, 67) sts.
SHAPE RIGHT NECK: Row 1 (RS): Using MC, k1, increase 1 st using Backward-Loop Cast-On (see page 126), k1, increase 1 using Backward-Loop Cast-On. Knit across.
Row 2 (WS): Using A, purl to last 2 sts, increase 1 st using Backward-Loop Cast-On, p1, increase 1 st using Backward-Loop Cast-On, purl last st.
Row 3: Using A, repeat Row 1.
Row 4: Using A, repeat Row 2.
Row 5: Using A, repeat Row 1.
Row 6: Using B, repeat Row 2.
Row 7: Using B, repeat Row 1.

Repeat Rows 2–7, choosing various colors for A and B until sts total 61 (73, 87, 99). Work even in Stripe Pattern until piece measures 4 (4½, 5, 5¾)" from beginning.

At beginning of next RS row, BO 20 (24, 28, 32) sts. Work even until piece measures 5½ (6¼, 7, 8)" from beginning. Place a marker here to distinguish Front from Back.

## Back

On next WS row, using MC, work for 1½ (1¾, 2, 2¼)". At beginning of next RS row, using the Backward-Loop method, CO 20 (24, 28, 32) sts.
Work until back measures 3½ (4¼, 5, 5¼)".
At beginning of next RS row, BO 4 (4, 6, 6) sts.
Work until back measures 7½ (8¼, 9, 10¾)".
At beginning of next RS row, CO 4 (4, 6, 6) sts.
Work until back measures 9½ (10¾, 12, 13¾)".

At beginning of next RS row, BO 20 (24, 28, 32) sts.

Work until back measures 11 (12½, 14, 16)". Place a marker here to distinguish Front from Back.

## Left Front

Beginning on next WS row, work Stripe Pattern in reverse color order as on Left Front.

Work until Left Front measures 1½ (1¾, 2, 2¼)".

On next RS row, CO 20 (24, 28, 32) sts.

Work until Left Front measures 3½ (4¼, 5, 5¼)".

### SHAPE LEFT NECK

Row 1 (WS): Purl to last 4 sts. P2tog twice.

Row 2 (RS): K2tog twice, knit across.

Repeat these 2 rows until 41 (49, 59, 67) sts remain.

On next WS row, using MC, purl across. Using MC, BO all sts.

## Finishing

Weave in all loose ends. Block vest, paying particular attention to the slope of the v-neck, where increases and decreases may cause it to curl. Sew shoulder seams.

### CROCHET EDGE

*Note: Take care when crocheting to produce an even edging. Too many stitches will cause the edge to pucker; too few will cause the edge to curl under. Add multiple sts when turning outer corners and reduce sts at inner corners for smooth curves.*

Rnd 1: Starting at bottom of vest, with crochet hook and MC, single crochet (sc) around entire bottom, Front edges, and neck opening.

Rnd 2: Slip st crochet around, evenly spacing 4 buttonhole loops on Left Front edge as follows:

BUTTONHOLE LOOPS: Chain 6 (or appropriate number to accommodate buttons), skip 2 sc sts, continue edging.

Repeat crochet edge around armholes. Sew on buttons opposite loops. ★

# Snow Cabin Goods

A SWEATER IS ONLY SOMETHING TO WEAR IF YOU THINK OF IT THAT WAY," KATHLEEN MITCHELL SAYS AS SHE DESCRIBES THE GARMENTS HAND-KNIT FOR HER WHOLESALE KNITWEAR COMPANY, SNOW CABIN GOODS, IN NEEDHAM, MASSACHUSETTS. "WHEN YOU REALIZE THAT IT WAS KNIT BY HAND WITH SKILL AND PATIENCE, THAT YOUR PURCHASE IMPACTS A LIFE BY PROVIDING INCOME FROM STEADY EMPLOYMENT, THEN YOUR DECISION TO WEAR IT IS AN ACTION THAT MAKES A DIFFERENCE." AND MAKING A DIFFERENCE—IN THIS CASE, IN THE LIVES OF WOMEN IN BOSNIA AND HERZEGOVINA, WHO KNIT AS A MEANS OF REBUILDING LIVES SHATTERED BY WAR—IS EXACTLY WHAT KATHLEEN IS DOING. ⊕ A savvy businesswoman with a penchant for knitted things, Kathleen founded Snow Cabin Goods in 1996, selling knitted goods imported from Scotland. The company took a geographic and philosophical turn in 1998, when Kathleen took a side trip to Bosnia after her honeymoon. "I had been thinking about the women in Bosnia all along," says Kathleen. "These were sophisticated, worldly European women who, before the war, had beautiful homes and rich, full lives. They were teachers, attorneys, secretaries, full-time moms." Then, in the war-torn years between 1992 and 1995, during which about 250,000 people died and more than 1 million were displaced, they lost almost everything.

The plight of these women made a deep impression on Kathleen, who decided that she could help. "I caught wind that women in Bosnia were knitting as part of postwar therapy," she says, and after a week and a half of "fishing around" in Sarajevo, with the help of aid agencies, the United Nations, and the World Bank, she found what she was looking for: a knitting support group run by a nongovernmental organization that was trying to shift from a nonprofit to a for-profit operation. By partnering with this group, she found not only a source of fresh and eager knitters, but also a way to help women struggling to live in a devastated country.

"The first time I was in Sarajevo, I got a very sick feeling," Kathleen says. "The military presence was still very clear. Cars were blown out, windows were boarded up, and parts of houses were missing. I thought, 'Wow—what have I gotten into?'" Then, she met the knitters. "Their lives have been demolished, and still they get up every day," Kathleen marvels. "They're so spirited, and they have every reason not to be."

The group of about a hundred women who knit for Snow Cabin Goods ranges in age from eighteen to seventy (most are in their late thirties and early forties), and they comprise a variety of ethnic backgrounds—Bosnian Muslim, Croatian, and Serbian. But their common plights override their differences, and their common work harks back to a time when such disparate groups coexisted. The Sarajevo group meets in what was once a private home; some knitters commute there together on what can be a two-hour journey. They travel in professional clothing; once there, about 8:30 in the morning, they change into sweatpants and handknit socks and "knit like mad," according to Kathleen. At the end of the day, about 4:30 or 5:00, they change back into their professional clothes to commute home. "Sarajevo is a very sophisticated European city," Kathleen points out, adding that keeping up a professional appearance, even if not required for work, is an important survival skill.

There were a few obstacles at first. Accustomed to living under Communist rule, the women were unused to making waves of any sort. "If there were problems—say, with yarn or a pattern—they didn't think it was appropriate to speak up," Kathleen recalls. "They didn't want to offend me." Once Kathleen communicated her expectations, however, the women rose to meet them immediately. "They want to do the right thing," she says. "I admire their willingness to learn, to adapt, to share their knowledge. When I give them a certain set of ideas, they may ask if I've considered something else. It becomes a collaboration." These days, the women knit under the supervision of a Bosnian woman who runs the group; Kathleen visits about once a year.

In return for their knitting, the women receive meaningful work, computer and English-language training, and a living wage, all of which is helping them reclaim their

> **There are scores of people waiting for someone just like us to come along; people who will appreciate our compassion, our encouragement, who will need our unique talents. Someone who will live a happier life merely because we took the time to share what we had to give.**
>
> **LEO BUSCAGLIA,**
> **author and professor**

lives, despite the slow recovery of their country and other setbacks. The original knitting group Kathleen partnered with, for example, has since disbanded. Many of those knitters were quickly absorbed by other cooperatives (several, such as Bosnian Handicrafts, have been formed in Bosnia since the war), but some of those original knitters still knit for Snow Cabin Goods. "These groups are learning to market themselves," she notes. "Many have proprietary yarns, so they are offering them as well as their own designs." Kathleen's voice can't hide her pride in their accomplishments. "They've come around 180 degrees in terms of their ability to come up with a collection, and their own product line, and their own yarn, and pull that together," she says.

Still, such advances don't change the fact that life in Bosnia—for these women in particular—is desperately hard. Unemployment is high and resettlement remains a serious problem (when one ethnic group overtook a particular town, members of the other groups were forced out of their homes and are now enduring long court struggles to get them back), and deep scars remain. "On my first visit to Sarajevo, the two women acting as managers for the knitting cooperative explained what had happened to them and their families during the war," Kathleen says. "They were pulled out of their homes in the middle of the night, witnessed their husbands being executed and their daughters raped, then fled to the woods in their nightclothes. I could not—and still cannot—believe that they survived and were actually hopeful about their futures." Yet with each day spent at the knitting center, with each stitch, these women dig themselves a little bit further out of the hole they've been put in, economically as well as emotionally.

In turn, the women have taught Kathleen lessons of the heart. "I have witnessed the strength of the human spirit to survive when literally all that is held dear is lost," she says. "I am reminded that each person has a goodness inside that thrives when nourished with love and attention."

In the face of their hardships, these women gather to knit daily, each moving forward in her own quiet, determined way. "They are indeed phenomenal heroes," muses Kathleen, and it's true: Each sweater knit is a product of hope, every stitch a prayer for peace. ★

**SUPPORTING SNOW CABIN GOODS**
For more information on Snow Cabin Goods, contact:

Snow Cabin Goods
946 Great Plain Avenue #249
Needham, MA 02492-3030
(781) 929-1076
www.snowcabingoods.com
info@snowcabingoods.com

For more information on Bosnian knitting cooperatives, visit www.bosnianhandicrafts.com, the website of Bosnian Handicrafts.

# Rwanda Knits

Seeing the country of Rwanda today, a visitor might never guess that in 1994 it was the scene of war and mass genocide that claimed the lives of more than 800,000 people, most of them men belonging to the Tutsi tribe. Since then, buildings and roads have been repaired, and the Rwandans—70 percent of whom, after the genocide, are women—seem to live normal lives. But these women have endured unimaginable hardship. They've seen husbands imprisoned and killed, and they've suffered the psychological, economic, and legal consequences of losing husbands in a very patriarchal—and very poor—society. HIV and AIDS are ever-present threats. Yet many of these women have made remarkable progress in rebuilding their lives, and in turn have helped rebuild their country. One of the ways they have done so is by knitting.

The knitting began when Cari Clement of Montpelier, Vermont, then president of the knitting machine company Bond America (now a division of Caron International, where Cari is fashion and design director), decided to help establish a women's cooperative that would use knitting to generate income for artisans in developing countries. From her newly formed nonprofit organization Fiber and Craft Entrepreneurial Development (FACED) Center, Cari wrote letters to several nongovernmental organizations, offering to donate hand-operated knitting machines and train knitters to use them. She received an enthusiastic response from USA for UNHCR (United Nations High Commission for Refugees), whose staff in Rwanda was eager to put them to use with Congolese and Burundi women living in refugee camps there.

In late 2002, Cari shipped sixty Ultimate Sweater Machines to Rwanda, along with one thousand skeins of donated yarn, which were distributed to refugee centers as

SUPPORTING RWANDA KNITS
For more information on Rwanda Knits and its supporting organizations, visit these websites:

Fiber and Craft Entrepreneurial Development (FACED) Center
www.fiberandcraft.org

Economic Development Imports (EDImports)
www.edimports.com

Bond America
www.bond-america.com

well as to women's cooperatives established by AVEGA (Association of Genocide Widows). In July 2003, she arrived in Rwanda to begin training. "The women learned quickly," she says with awe. In just four days, more than one hundred women, none of whom spoke English, learned to use the machines. On a subsequent trip, Cari returned to one of the knitting centers to find the walls lined with completed sweaters, the results of months of "practicing."

The knitting program became known as Rwanda Knits, and since its inception, the women's knitting has reached the U.S. market through Economic Development Imports (EDImports), a New York company that sells handmade goods from women in postconflict countries through independent boutiques, online catalogs, and other retailers. "We pay the artisans a fair wage, well above the market there," says Liz Wald, the company's founder, adding that a portion of the profits is returned to the cooperatives. As a result, the Rwandan knitters are able to pay their children's school fees, move toward financial independence, and have some fun. "Africa's a very social culture," Cari says. "The women enjoy working together, despite their cultural differences." In the cooperatives, Tutsi widows work easily alongside Huti women, whose husbands are imprisoned for taking part in the Tutsi genocide.

The knitted products themselves reflect the hopeful spirit of the land in which they were knit. They include a hand-embroidered Peace Poncho, Unity Wrap, and Scarves for Peace, all knit with South African mohair. Liz makes a point of using materials native to the region and designs that reflect local cultures, with great success. "These are high-quality, handmade goods that have a great story," says Liz. "People don't buy them out of charity or pity."

A story behind one product in particular, the On Their Way Poncho, illustrates the positive impact Rwanda Knits has made. In late 2004, this poncho was presented to Nane Annan, wife of U.N. Secretary-General Kofi Annan, at the United Nations launch of the International Year of Microcredit, an effort to support programs that promote economic sustainability in developing countries. The poncho was made by a twenty-five-year-old survivor of the Rwandan genocide, Esperance Nyirarusimbi. Prior to working with Rwanda Knits, Esperance had lost her entire family, had no form of income, and was surviving on subsistence farming. Now she makes a living as a knitter and travels throughout the country training other knitters, bringing skills and hope to other survivors.

"There are so many opportunities for growth in Rwanda after the rebuilding," says Liz, adding that a high priority in Rwanda is keeping the peace that has been restored. "When more people are working and supporting themselves," she says, "there's less chance of violence. You can visually see the difference in villages where people have work opportunities. They are clean, the people are well dressed, and the children are in school."

The future for the hardworking knitters of Rwanda Knits is only getting brighter. In 2005, the program received a grant from USAID (United States Agency for International Development) that enabled thirteen new knitting cooperatives to be established throughout Rwanda. Each item knit represents an opportunity for a Rwandan or refugee woman, a prospect that brings joy to all involved. "I have always known that making beautiful things lifts the spirit and offers hope," says Cari. "In Rwanda, I really saw it happen."

## Kenana Knitters

"Our knitters are some of the happiest women in the world!" declares Gloria Delaney. She's referring to the 200-plus ladies who make up Kenana Knitters, a group of women in rural Njoro, Kenya, who are gaining income, camaraderie, health care, and more by hand-knitting garments and adorable stuffed animals—their specialty—for Western markets. Any knitter would envy their work environment. The women spend the day together knitting on blankets spread on the grass. Their babies snooze close by in the shade, surrounded by soft, knitted animals. The air rings with their laughter and chatter.

Kenana Knitters was founded in 1998 by Paddy Nightingale and her husband, Bruce, who together run the Kenana Farm. Paddy began the knitting program in hopes of supplying much-needed income to women whose husbands worked on the farm. Traditionally, women in this part of Kenya stay home, raising children and keeping house while their husbands work. But in a largely agricultural work environment, where the unemployment rate can reach 60 to 80 percent, a single income is rarely enough, and husbands often aren't willing to share what they do earn with their wives. The knitting program offers women a direct and fair income of their own, allowing them to pay their children's school fees, buy food, and pay medical bills. In addition, the Kenana Knitters receive health care and

> **SUPPORTING KENANA KNITTERS**
> For more information on Kenana Knitters and to purchase their products, visit www.kenanaknitters.com and www.kenanausa.com.

> **"**
> **Never doubt that a small group of thoughtful, committed citizens can change the world. Indeed, it is the only thing that ever has.**
> **"**
>
> MARGARET MEAD

AIDS exams through a facility on the farm, reading lessons through the group's literacy program, and even eyeglasses.

All the fiber used for the stuffed animals and other products they knit is hand-spun from wool raised on Kenana Farm, and is either knit in its natural colors or hand-dyed from the flowers, leaves, and roots of plants grown on the farm. The whimsical African menagerie that emerges from the needles—monkeys, bears, zebras, lions, and more—reflects not only the natural beauty of the materials, but also the happiness of the knitters, who sign their names to every finished product.

"They are good at what they do, and they *love* their work," says Gloria, who sells the stuffed animals and other goods to U.S. retailers like Coldwater Creek, Anthropologie, and ABC Carpet & Home through her importing company, Dwelling, LLC. "Their self-pride is beautiful to witness."

## Lantern Moon

For knitters, it's hard not to covet the knitting products made by Lantern Moon. The beautiful yarn we collect is showcased in their colorful woven baskets, and stitches glide smoothly along their silky exotic-wood needles. But as pleasant as these tools are to behold and use, it's the story behind them that brings their true beauty to life. All of Lantern Moon's products—baskets and needles, bags, needle cases, and more—are handmade by Vietnamese producers who, in turn, gain skills, income, and self-reliance.

Co-owners Bruce Feller and Sharon and Joel Woodcock began Lantern Moon in 2001, shortly after the Woodcocks moved to Portland, Oregon, from Ho Chi Min City, where Joel had been working for a small American company since 1996. While there, Sharon had befriended two Vietnamese women, social workers who helped women

in rural villages use their traditional crafts—particularly basket-weaving—to gain self-sufficiency. The setup was a win-win situation for the artisans; they could remain in their own homes and villages, work while watching their children, and receive fair compensation. "I loved the Vietnamese people," Sharon says of the artisans she met in the villages she visited. "They're so warm, and their handwork is so beautiful. They're very skilled." Yet Sharon was also struck by the extreme poverty in which they lived, and the lengths to which many people would go—leaving their families and traveling to distant cities—to find work. Hoping she, too, could help them, Sharon brought several of their handwoven rice baskets, traditionally used to carry rice from the paddies, to the United States when she and Joel moved back, intending to seek out a U.S. market for them.

Upon moving to Portland and joining forces with Bruce, who had previous experience in the gift market, the Woodcocks began looking for potential retailers, focusing primarily on home decor and quilt stores. But the strongest interest came from the local yarn store, Yarn Garden, where the baskets were snapped up by the dozens. "We found out that knitters love baskets," said Bruce—no surprise to those of us who knit. The owner of Yarn Garden, Linda Carter, helped them get into the national yarn market, where the baskets were an immediate hit.

As the team at Lantern Moon brainstormed new product ideas, many inspired by pieces the Vietnamese artisans traditionally wove, they found more and more producers in villages across Vietnam who could be trained to make the baskets. "As in many cultures," says Sharon, "their handwork reflects nature and the natural colors around them. When I visit them, they show me their baskets, and I adapt them to U.S. markets," often simply by tweaking color choices and adding linings. As the popularity of knitting in the United States skyrocketed, and an

actual knitting-needle shortage ensued, the Lantern Moon collection grew to include hand-crafted needles, and the company established a needle factory through a Vietnamese business contact. The needles are crafted through a thirty-step process, much of which is done by hand. The factory provides opportunities to yet another Vietnamese village—more than 100 people are employed there full-time—and the working conditions are exceptional.

All the materials used for Lantern Moon products, with the exception of the rosewood and ebony used for some of the needles, are indigenous to Vietnam and grow there abundantly. The rosewood and ebony are obtained from Indonesia, and are purchased from registered sources that ensure the harvesting is legitimate and the trees are replenished. In every aspect of their business, those at Lantern Moon strive to maintain a natural balance with the earth, the people, and their traditions.

"We try to create a place where families and communities come together, where culture is preserved," says Sharon of all the villages participating with Lantern Moon. "The baskets, especially, honor a kind of circle of creativity," she adds. "They're passed from women in Vietnam to women in the United States who share an appreciation for handwork, a love of doing things with their hands."

Chapter
Three

# Peace
## —AT—
# Home

# Shawl Ministry

IN 1998, VICTORIA GALO AND JANET BRISTOW FOUND A SIMPLE, HEARTFELT WAY TO REACH OUT TO PEOPLE THEY KNEW WHO WERE IN NEED OF PEACE: THEY KNIT THEM SHAWLS. IN SO DOING, AND WITHOUT ANY IDEA OF WHAT THEY WERE STARTING, THEY LAUNCHED AN INCREDIBLY FAR-REACHING KNITTING MOVEMENT—THE SHAWL MINISTRY. THE INTENT BEHIND THIS MINISTRY IS NOT JUST TO KNIT SHAWLS OF COMFORT FOR PEOPLE IN SORROW OR SHAWLS OF JOY FOR THOSE IN CELEBRATION, BUT TO DO SO MINDFULLY, LOVINGLY, AND PRAYER-FULLY. THE ONE NEEDING COMFORT IS SOOTHED NOT ONLY BY THE WARM FOLDS OF A HAND-KNIT SHAWL, BUT ALSO BY THE LOVE, THOUGHTS, AND PRAYERS OF THE KNITTER, WHETHER A CLOSE FRIEND OR PERFECT STRANGER. ✺ An irrepressible spirit underlies this movement, which has spread across the country and beyond. Everyone, it seems, is making "prayer shawls"—from neighbors in Brownsville, Minnesota (population 517), to women in a self-help program in Uganda. Shawls are being knit for close friends with cancer, for mothers with new babies, for the victims of 2005's Hurricane Katrina, and for families in Beslan, Russia, who lost children in the 2004 siege of a school there.

It took a lot of energy—good, positive energy—to initiate such a widespread and popular movement. And if you meet Vicky and Janet, who together compose the heart of Shawl Ministry, you'll see just where that energy comes from. A few minutes into a conversation on the Shawl Ministry, their eyes light up, they move to the edge of their seats, and they begin finishing each other's sentences. Their voices and words are filled with excitement, but also with wonder at this thing they have created and the myriad ways it is affecting people, both those who knit the shawls and those who receive them. "We didn't mean for this to happen," says Janet. "We were just reaching out to those around us. To me, it's proof it came from beyond."

As divine inspirations often do, this one came in humble packaging. Vicky and Janet are two ordinary women. They have jobs and families, they are members of churches (one Catholic, one Congregational), and in their spare time they knit. But in 1997, both were seeking something more—a new perspective on God and themselves, a perspective with a different focus than the traditions they'd been raised with, one that spoke to them uniquely as women. This desire led them to the Women's Leadership Institute at the Hartford Seminary in Hartford,

Connecticut, an intensive nine-month course in women's spirituality. Here, they learned to see God in a new light—as a nurturing, comforting, mothering, and creative being—and to see those same divine qualities in themselves and each other. "It was a gradual awakening, an expanding of views," Janet says of discovering what she calls the feminine face of God. "I wanted that course to last forever."

"Upon receiving our certificates," Vicky adds, "we were challenged with the question, 'How are we going to take what we've learned out into the world?'" Acting upon an urge to "get sacred with my hands," Vicky started by knitting a shawl for a friend who was going through a divorce. She showed it to Janet, who was reminded of a Mexican serape a friend of hers wore to pray. They brought Vicky's finished shawl to their women's group, where each woman wrapped herself in it and gave it a blessing before it was given to the recipient. "The shawl seemed to be a metaphor for what we had just been through in the course," says Janet, "a physical symbol of a God who holds you, comforts you, and mothers you."

Using knitting as the medium for taking what they had learned out into the world, they began making more shawls for women they knew, infusing each one with their prayers, thoughts, and hopes for the recipient. "Vicky and I were so inspired by the Women's Institute, so ready to see what was next for us, that the pieces just fell together," Janet says. "We didn't have a business plan. Other knitters saw this was something they could do, and a grassroots movement began." Like ripples in a lake, the shawl movement began spreading, its goodwill, thoughts, and prayers carried back and forth from knitter to recipient on the gentle waves.

"Knitting is very connected to the feminine," Vicky observes, "and maybe this is the way the divine feminine is working through us." Which may beg the question:

★ ★ ★ ★ ★ ★ ★ ★ ★ ★ ★

For centuries, women have been wrapping themselves in shawls for warmth and protection, comfort and beauty. Babies have been bundled in them, too. In the Jewish culture, men use four-cornered, fringed shawls called *tallith* during prayers. "A shawl is universal," Janet says. "Every culture wraps itself in cloth."

★ ★ ★ ★ ★ ★ ★ ★ ★ ★ ★

Maintaining the Shawl Ministry is no small job. The Shawl Ministry website receives 1,000 hits a day, and Vicky and Janet personally answer every single e-mail they receive. But for them, this is work that fuels rather than drains.

★ ★ ★ ★ ★ ★ ★ ★ ★ ★ ★

Is God a knitter? "Absolutely!" both women declare, laughingly. Janet recalls the Bible verse, "You knitted me in my mother's womb," and adds, "We are being knitted by God all the time. God does it all—basket weaver, potter, the ultimate craftsperson!"

The shawls that knitters are thoughtfully making as part of the Shawl Ministry are commonly known as "prayer shawls" but are also called "comfort shawls," "mantles," and, fittingly, "peace shawls." The original pattern for a Shawl Ministry shawl (though knitters may knit and give shawls in any pattern they choose) is a simple one Janet designed using repetitions of knit 3, purl 3 in a modified seed stitch, suggesting that knitters "plant" their prayers as they work. The use of the number three is no accident, either. "In the Christian faith," Janet and Vicky write on their website, "the number three, symbolized by the Trinity, has come to mean wholeness." And they point out more universal trinities: the stages of a woman's life (maiden, mother, crone); time (past, present, future); human makeup (body, mind, spirit); and existence itself (birth, life, death). In the Chinese tradition, three is a perfect number, and it is the sacred number of the woman in Mayan culture.

The blessings brought about by the prayer shawls are also threefold. First, says Vicky, shawls honor the shawl makers: "As women," she says, "we make handcrafts, we bake or crochet, and we say, 'Oh, it's nothing, just something I made.' But it's important not to dismiss what we can create. You took time to make this. That is a blessing; that is prayer." The process of knitting the shawl

### KNITTING FOR THE SHAWL MINISTRY

• To knit a prayer shawl—or comfort shawl or peace shawl—follow the pattern on page 54 or use one of your own choosing. Visit www.shawlministry.com for other patterns and shawl knitting tips.

• If you are knitting a shawl for someone you know, personalize it by using a color meaningful to the recipient or by adorning it with beads, charms, or other objects. These may be sewn on the shawl or tied into the fringe.

• If you don't have a particular recipient in mind, consider knitting shawls for patients in hospitals, residents in nursing homes, or others you know of—perhaps through your faith community—who are in need. Or save the shawl until the recipient "appears" in your life.

• As you knit, think about the person it's for. You may choose to pray, meditate on sacred writings, or simply send good wishes. Visit the Shawl Ministry website for prayers and other ideas for mindful knitting.

• If you are knitting as part of a Shawl Ministry group, consider beginning your knitting gatherings with a blessing, prayer, or thought for meditation or discussion. Keep spirit at the center. If you'd like to start a Shawl Ministry program, visit the Shawl Ministry website to learn how.

• For additional information, visit www.shawlministry.com or send an e-mail to shawlministry@yahoo.com.

invites the knitter into a sacred space—an artful, meditative state in which she can still herself and rejuvenate. "How many of us don't take the time to clear our minds and let that creative flow in?" asks Vicky. "As women, we need to take care of ourselves first, center ourselves before we have to go back out into the world. Knitting is one of the best ways to do that."

Second, and perhaps most obviously, the shawls bless the recipients. "What you put into your passion can't help but be received at the other end," says Vicky, recalling a shawl she knit early in the ministry for a woman who had lost her two children in a car accident. "I blotted my own tears with that shawl," says Vicky, recalling how she filled the piece with her own sympathy and heartbreak, something her words alone could not express.

"When the shawl is passed on to the receiver, it's a grace-filled moment for the giver as well because a part of herself goes with the shawl," says Janet. And this is true whether a shawl is given to a close friend or to someone the knitter has never met. In fact, observes Vicky, there's a certain serendipity that takes place when you're knitting a shawl with no particular recipient in mind. "When you open your heart," she says, "people who need shawls will start showing up in your life."

And finally, the community that so often gathers around the knitting of these shawls is blessed by them. The spirit of the Shawl Ministry, as Vicky and Janet have created it, is meant to be as inclusive as possible, blind to political stance, ethnicity, and especially religion. When Vicky and Janet offer workshops about starting Shawl Ministry groups— most of which are formed within churches—they emphasize the importance of inviting in knitters from the community, regardless of their religious backgrounds.

"Knitting transcends all differences," says Vicky. "It brings together different people of different faith traditions. It begins an ecumenical dialogue." Knitting the prayer shawls offers knitters an opportunity to open their minds about God, about each other, and about beliefs different from their own. In a world where faith so often is divisive, highlighting differences and encouraging schisms, the Shawl Ministry is building bridges.

"All are welcome in the Shawl Ministry," Janet emphasizes. "It's meant to be an outpouring of unconditional love. It's the workings of the Holy Spirit—or whatever you want to call that energy." Call it what you wish: God, spirit, the divine mother, or simply the collective goodwill and heartfelt prayers of thousands of knitters. "It feels like we're being guided," says Janet. "Sometimes I feel I'm just along for the ride. The Shawl Ministry constantly evolves, changes, expands—we're running to keep up with it. And it'll keep on evolving," she adds. "It's a living thing." ★

# Shawl Ministry Prayer Shawl

## —DESIGNED BY VICTORIA GALO & JANET BRISTOW—

BECAUSE MAKING A PRAYER—OR PEACE—SHAWL IS MEANT TO BE A SPIRITUAL PRACTICE, FOUNDERS AND SHAWL DESIGNERS VICTORIA GALO AND JANET BRISTOW ENCOURAGE YOU TO OFFER A BLESSING, PRAYER, OR WISH BEFORE YOU BEGIN KNITTING, DEDICATING THE WORK OF YOUR HANDS AND YOUR INTENTIONS FOR THE RECEIVER. YOU MIGHT ALSO LIGHT A CANDLE, PLAY SOFT MUSIC, OR EVEN MEDITATE.

THIS SHAWL PATTERN IS INTENTIONALLY VERSATILE. THE BROKEN GARTER-STITCH PATTERN, BASED ON MULTIPLES OF THREE, CAN BE ADJUSTED TO CREATE WIDER OR NARROWER SHAWLS, DEPENDING ON THE NUMBER OF STITCHES USED (THREE OPTIONS ARE GIVEN HERE). THE LOOK OF THE SHAWL CAN ALSO BE ALTERED WITH NEEDLE SIZE: USE THE SMALLER NEEDLE SUGGESTED FOR A DENSE LOOK WITH MORE STITCH DEFINITION, OR THE LARGER NEEDLE FOR A MORE LOOSELY KNIT, FLOWING SHAWL.

FINISHED MEASUREMENTS
Approximately 18 (19, 20)" wide by 58" long

YARN: Approximately 555 yards bulky-weight novelty yarn

*Sample shown in Classic Elite Yarns Bravo (40% rayon/35% mohair/13% silk/6% wool/6% nylon)*

NEEDLES: One pair straight needles or 24" circular (circ) needle size US 11 (8 mm) or one pair straight needles or 24" circular (circ) needle size US 13 (9 mm) *Change needle size if necessary to obtain correct gauge.*

NOTIONS: Crochet hook (any medium to large size), beads, charms, or other embellishments (optional)

GAUGE: 12 sts and 16 rows = 4" (10 cm) in shawl pattern stitch

NOTE: To ensure enough yarn remains to make fringe, cut fringe from your last skein before you begin knitting with it.

## Shawl

CO 54 (57, 60) sts (this pattern will work with any multiple of 3 stitches).
Row 1: *K3, p3, repeat from * across.
Row 2: Knit the purl sts and purl the knit sts as they face you.

*Note: This creates a Broken Garter st pattern and should not look like ribbing.*

*With even numbers of sts, Row 2 will always begin with p3. With odd numbers, it will always begin with k3.*

Repeat Rows 1–2 until shawl measures 58" or desired length (approximately wrist to wrist). BO all sts knitwise.

## Fringe

Cut remaining yarn in lengths twice the length of the desired fringe. For example, for a 12" fringe, cut 24" lengths. Cut 54 (57, 60) lengths per side, one for each st on the needle.

To attach fringe, fold one length of yarn in half. Insert crochet hook into the first stitch on either the cast-on or bound-off edge, pull up a loop by catching the length of fringe at its center point, and pull the loose ends through the loop. Pull tight. Repeat for remaining stitches on the cast-on and bound-off edges. Trim fringe even if necessary.

If you choose, you may further embellish the fringe by tying on beads, charms, or other ornaments with symbolic meaning for the recipient. ★

## Sheila's Shawls

It wasn't your everyday fashion show. No pouting waifs stalked the catwalks sporting impossible-to-wear constructions. Instead, the featured haute couture at this event was the shawl: delicate lace shawls, humble comfort shawls, shawls honoring countries across the globe, shawls named for brave women like Harriet Tubman and Susan B. Anthony. All of them were glorious and handmade, and all were wrapped around models of varied ages, shapes, and sizes who twirled their way across the stage in a high-spirited celebration of creativity and social action. Yet for all its festivity, the Sheila Shawl Extravaganza, held at the University of Minnesota in June 2004, had at its center a sobering impetus—the ongoing fight against domestic violence and the memory of one of its foremost crusaders, the late Sheila Wellstone.

On October 25, 2002, Sheila Wellstone, champion for domestic violence awareness, was killed in a plane crash, along with her husband, Minnesota Senator Paul Wellstone. For many, it was impossible to accept that these two tireless advocates for public well-being were gone.

Janet Hagberg, a friend of Sheila's and a fellow domestic violence activist, soothed her feelings of loss by wrapping herself in a prayer shawl she'd knit as part of the Shawl Ministry program (see page 50). Enveloped in her shawl, Janet felt a gentle, reassuring presence. "It was as if Sheila were in the room with me," she remembers. "I thought, if wearing this shawl can give me this much comfort, what might it do for a woman mourning the loss of a friend, sister, or daughter who's been a casualty of domestic violence?"

As cofounder and director of the Silent Witness National Initiative, a Minneapolis-based center for domestic violence prevention, Janet knows the statistics well: Each day in the United States, about three women are killed by their husbands or boyfriends (though that number, she's happy to report, is on the decline). Through Silent Witness, Janet and others work to promote research on domestic violence and to raise awareness of the issue, chiefly through displays of life-size red wooden cutouts in the outline of a woman's body. Each cutout bears a breastplate telling the name and story of a woman murdered by a husband or loved one. These displays have appeared in exhibits in every state and in seventeen other countries.

Her prayer shawl—and the enduring efforts of Sheila Wellstone—gave Janet a new idea for reaching out. Operating in much the same manner as the Shawl Ministry program, and with permission to use their basic shawl pattern, Janet began coordinating the knitting and distribution of Sheila's Shawls to anyone affected by domestic violence (Paul's Scarves are knit for men who have lost loved ones). The simple shawls are knit and donated by volunteers around the country, then shipped to several regional Silent Witness distribution centers. "The shawls," says Janet, "are a way to use the beauty of women's art to bring comfort to women in dire situations."

The Sheila Shawl Extravaganza—the upbeat fund-raiser at the University of Minnesota—was a high-profile extension of this quieter movement. In the months leading up to the event, seventy-five shawls were designed and created by talented knitters, crocheters, and weavers (Janet knit two of them herself) and displayed in an exhibit at the university's Goldstein Museum of Design. "I wanted this event to make a statement that would be seen and felt, not just heard, like a statistic," says Janet. "Art raises the issue to a new level. It touches the heart, raises passion in a way a statistic cannot."

At auction, the exhibited shawls raised more than $40,000

to endow the Sheila Wellstone fellowship in the University of Minnesota School of Social Work; the fellowship is earmarked for students pursuing studies in the prevention of domestic violence. Fittingly, the shawl that caught the eye of the highest bidder was "Sheila's Shawl" by Marcia Avner, Paul Wellstone's chief staff member and Sheila's closest associate. Worked in sections of mauve, purple, and moss green—the colors in Sheila's favorite dress—the soft woolen shawl reflects the warm and wonderful woman Marcia remembers.

---

**KNITTING FOR SHEILA'S SHAWLS**

• To knit a shawl, follow the pattern for the Prayer Shawl on page 54 or use one of your own choosing. Other patterns can be found at www.silentwitness.net by clicking on the "Sheila Wellstone Shawl" link.

• The purpose of knitting a healing shawl is to weave good thoughts, healing, hope, love, and peace into the shawl so that it will comfort and warm the recipient. Be reflective or offer a prayer for the recipient as you knit.

• Visit www.silentwitness.net for a listing of shawl distribution points. A $10 contribution to help cover shipping costs is appreciated.

For more information on the Silent Witness National Initiative, contact:

Janet Hagberg
Silent Witness National
   Headquarters
20 Second Street NE
Suite 1101
Minneapolis, MN 55413
(612) 623-0999
www.silentwitness.net
info@silentwitness.net

# Warm Up America!

THE MOTHER OF ALL KNITTING CHARITIES MAY BE WARM UP AMERICA!, THE EFFORT TO BLANKET PEOPLE IN NEED ACROSS THE COUNTRY WITH HANDKNIT AFGHANS. FEW KNITTERS WITH A CHARITABLE BENT HAVE NOT HEARD OF IT, AND THERE'S A GOOD CHANCE—WHAT WITH ITS PUBLICITY ON TV TALK SHOWS, PLUGS IN NUMEROUS KNITTING AND NON-KNITTING PUBLICATIONS, AND CELEBRITY BACKERS LIKE ROSIE O'DONNELL AND VANNA WHITE—THAT MANY WHO'VE NEVER PICKED UP A KNITTING NEEDLE HAVE HEARD OF IT TOO. WHAT MIGHT SURPRISE EVEN THE MOST DEDICATED KNITTER-FOR-PEACE, THOUGH, IS WHAT A SIMPLE, GRASSROOTS, HAND-TO-HAND EFFORT IT BEGAN AS—AND STILL IS. ⊕ The mother of Warm Up America! is Evie Rosen, who began the charity in 1991 at The Knitting Nook, her yarn shop in Wausau, Wisconsin, in an attempt to alleviate not only homelessness in America, but also the leftover balls of yarn that accumulate so rapidly in knitters' stashes. Evie's idea was straightforward and practical: Use that leftover yarn to knit squares, which could be collected and sewn together into afghans for those who have lost their homes. "The two just meshed together," she says.

Evie is seventy-eight years old now, a woman with a soft voice but a snappy wit, and although she's closed The Knitting Nook and claims to have retired from Warm Up America!—the Craft Yarn Council of America has run it since 1994—she remains very much involved, collecting the afghans that still magically appear on her back porch, "making snide comments" (as CYCA executive director Mary Colucci teases), and generally keeping everyone on their toes. Mary has been Evie's sidekick in the Warm Up America! movement since its inception.

The very name *Warm Up America!* suggests that Evie's idea, despite its small-town start, was always meant to be ambitious and far-reaching. Even so, Evie's intent was to keep the program simple, a real grassroots effort in which neighbors helped neighbors, particularly those in homeless shelters, women's shelters, and the like. Early on a *Milwaukee Journal Sentinel* reporter caught wind of Warm Up America! and wrote a feature story on it. Once that was published, "letters began pouring in from all over Wisconsin," Evie says. "And we Wisconsinites have relatives all over the country. Word spread very rapidly." Shortly afterward, another article appeared in *Crafts* magazine, the premier publication of the industry at the time. "From there," Mary Colucci says, "it just exploded."

The problem with founding a community charity effort that suddenly goes national is that it can be difficult to keep up. In the beginning, the afghans went to families and individuals in Wausau and greater Wisconsin who had lost their homes, whether to fire, natural disaster, or financial difficulties. "People were getting a lot of benefit out of it—local people in need, the knitters," Evie says. "The only thing that *didn't* benefit terribly was my back porch," which became filled with surplus afghans.

Afghans—fully completed ones as well as bags full of squares—were coming in from everywhere. They were being knit by customers who gathered in Evie's shop, by elderly knitters in retirement homes, by corporate types on their lunch hours in New York City, and by children in schools, 4-H groups, and Scout groups. In the pre-Internet early nineties, the effort

was publicized efficiently by word of mouth. Evie acted as the collection and distribution point, gathering squares, bagging them in batches of forty-nine (the number needed for a full-size afghan), coordinating the volunteers who diligently stitched them together, and distributing them to shelters who contacted her. She was soon overwhelmed.

Eventually, Warm Up America! came under the umbrella of the CYCA, where it remains today as a foundation with nonprofit status. But despite its fifteen-plus years of existence, it operates in the same way as it began, as a hands-on, neighbor-to-neighbor effort.

Evie remembers the days when distribution of the afghans was completely up to her and Mary. "We stockpiled them," Evie says, "and when there was a large national market somewhere, Mary would make arrangements to donate them to a homeless shelter in that city." She chuckles. "I was in New York City once with Mary," she recalls, "and we took a van loaded

★ ★ ★ ★ ★ ★ ★ ★ ★ ★ ★

Anyone who has knit an afghan, or who has a half-knit afghan buried in a closet, knows what an undertaking it is. Hence the brilliance of Evie's strategy: Gather enough squares knit in a uniform size—seven by nine inches, to be exact—then find someone to assemble them, and no one is faced with the daunting task of completing an entire afghan.

★ ★ ★ ★ ★ ★ ★ ★ ★ ★ ★

The success of Warm Up America! is partly due to the manageability of the knitting, and partly because it allows knitters to make a difference, no matter how big or small their contribution. Each square counts.

★ ★ ★ ★ ★ ★ ★ ★ ★ ★ ★

with afghans out on the streets and gave them to homeless people. It was a unique experience. Some people were very grateful; some were quite suspicious. Some were asleep, and we covered them up."

Warm Up America! knitters are, and always have been, encouraged to keep their efforts local by knitting, assembling, and distributing the afghans in their own communities. "Evie never wanted something that was only a centralized program," Mary says. "And it's very gratifying—very fulfilling—to be able to do something for your neighbors."

Still, for those who cannot contribute locally, CYCA acts as the collection point for completed afghans, as well as for the individual squares. These usually amount to several dozen boxes of squares a week (several hundred if there's been mention in the media). Volunteers local to CYCA's Ranlo, North Carolina, office, including women at the Lucile Tatum Extension Homemakers Center and other community groups,

wield the needles that stitch those thousands of squares together.

At Knit-Outs, CYCA-sponsored knitting events held annually in several U.S. cities, knitters are invited to bring completed Warm Up America! squares, and they do, sometimes by the bagful. Participants are also invited to pick up needles and sew the blankets together—every stitch helps. CYCA maintains a database of shelters and Red Cross chapters nationwide that regularly request afghans, and the need for them is constant, particularly when natural disasters hit.

"We love it; we need it," Mary says of the inundation of squares. "We always have a waiting list." But just as there seems to be an endless need for Warm Up America! afghans, so too is there an endless supply. "I think it's just a bottomless thing," says Evie. "There's something about loaves and fishes. . . ." ★

# Warm Up America! Afghan

IF YOU ARE ABLE TO COORDINATE EFFORTS, THIS AFGHAN CAN BE A WONDERFUL COMMUNITY PROJECT. IF YOU AREN'T PART OF A GROUP, OR DON'T HAVE TIME TO KNIT MORE THAN A FEW SQUARES, THE VOLUNTEERS AT WARM UP AMERICA! HEADQUARTERS CAN COMBINE THEM WITH SQUARES RECEIVED FROM OTHERS. FOR EASE IN ASSEMBLY, MAKE SURE THE SQUARES MEASURE AS CLOSE TO 7" BY 9" AS POSSIBLE. ADJUST NEEDLE SIZE—OR EVEN THE NUMBER OF STITCHES—TO ACHIEVE THE NECESSARY DIMENSIONS.

FINISHED MEASUREMENTS
Finished square: 7" by 9"
Assembled afghan: Approximately 49" wide by 63" long

YARN: Approximately 60 yards washable worsted-weight yarn per square

*Shown in Brown Sheep Company Lamb's Pride Super Wash (100% superwash wool)*

NEEDLES: One pair straight needles size US 7 (4.5 mm)
*Change needle size if necessary to obtain correct gauge.*

NOTIONS: Yarn needle

GAUGE: 20 sts and 28 rows = 4" (10 cm) in Stockinette stitch (St st) (Gauge may vary with other pattern stitches.)

## Garter Stitch Square
CO 35 sts.
Knit every row until piece measures 9" from beginning. BO all sts.

## Stockinette Stitch Square
CO 35 sts.
Row 1: Knit.
Row 2: Purl.
Repeat these 2 rows until piece measures 9" from beginning. BO all sts.

## Seed Stitch Square
CO 35 sts.
Row 1:*K1, p1, repeat from * across to last st, k1.
Row 2: Purl the knit sts, and knit the purl sts as they face you.
Repeat Row 2 until piece measures 9" from beginning. BO all sts.

## Moss Stitch Square
CO 35 sts.
Row 1: *K1, p1, repeat from * across to last st, k1.
Row 2: Purl the purl sts and knit the knit sts as they face you.
Row 3: Purl the knit sts and knit the purl sts as they face you.
Row 4: Repeat Row 2.
Repeat Rows 1–4 until piece measures 9" from beginning. BO all sts.

## Checkerboard Square
CO 35 sts.
Row 1: *K5, p5, repeat from * across to last 5 sts, k5.
Row 2: *P5, k5, repeat from * across to last 5 sts, p5.
Row 3: Repeat Row 1.
Row 4: Repeat Row 2.
Row 5: Repeat Row 1.
Row 6: Repeat Row 2.
Row 7: *P5, k5, repeat from * across to last 5 sts, p5.
Row 8: *K5, p5, repeat from * across to last 5 sts, k5.
Row 9: Repeat Row 7.
Row 10: Repeat Row 8.
*(continued on next page)*

# Warm Up America! Afghan (continued)

Row 11: Repeat Row 7.
Row 12: Repeat Row 8.
Repeat Rows 1–12 until piece measures 9" from beginning. BO all sts.

## Eyelet Stitch Square
CO 35 sts.
Row 1: Knit.
Row 2: Purl.
Row 3: *K2, k2tog, yo; repeat from * across to last 3 sts, k3.
Row 4: Purl.
Row 5: Knit.
Row 6: Purl.
Row 7: *K2tog, yo, k2; repeat from * across to last st, k1.
Row 8: Purl.
Repeat Rows 1–8 until piece measures 9" from beginning. BO all sts.

## Garter Stitch Ridge Square (horizontal stripes)
CO 35 sts.
Row 1: Knit.
Row 2: Purl.
Row 3: Knit.
Row 4: Purl.
Rows 5–10: Purl.
Repeat Rows 1–10 until piece measures 9" from beginning. BO all sts.

## Ribbed Square (vertical stripes)
CO 36 sts.
Row 1: P1 (edge st), *k2, p2; repeat from * across to last st, p1.
Row 2: K1 (edge st), *p2, k2; repeat from * across to last st, k1.
Repeat Rows 1–2 until piece measures 9" from beginning. BO all sts.

## Assembly
Complete 49 squares in a variety of colors and patterns. Block all squares and lay them out as desired, 7 squares wide by 7 squares long, alternating colors and stitch patterns. Sew together with whipstitch or Mattress stitch. Alternatively, crochet the squares together, or crochet a border around the edge of each square, and then sew or crochet them together. ★

# Hugs for Homeless Animals

ON EARTH DAY 2005, ERIC ROBINSON AND HER HIGH SCHOOL STUDENTS AT VERMONT ACADEMY IN SAXTONS RIVER, VERMONT, SPENT THE DAY KNITTING. ALL OF THE TWELVE STUDENTS WHO GATHERED THAT DAY WERE BRAND-NEW KNITTERS—BUT NO MATTER. THE RECIPIENTS OF THEIR FINISHED PIECES—SIMPLE SQUARES LATER ASSEMBLED INTO SMALL BLAN-KETS—DIDN'T MIND THE AWKWARD ROWS AND DROPPED STITCHES. TO THE DOGS AND CATS AT THE LOCAL HUMANE SOCIETY, THESE BLANKETS, CALLED SNUGGLES, PROVIDED A SOFT ALTERNATIVE TO HARD FLOORS AND STAINLESS STEEL CAGING. ⊕ The Snuggles Project is a component of Hugs for Homeless Animals, a nonprofit organization in Oregon that provides knitted, crocheted, and fabric blankets to animal shelters nationwide, as well as support

programs that connect the public with animal-care organizations. Rae French began Hugs for Homeless Animals in 1996 when, after trying to bring a stray cat to an animal shelter, she was faced with the sobering realities of an animal's life and death there. Rae kept the cat and strived to

improve the quality of life for those animals who remained in shelters. Generally speaking, many more animals are given to shelters than can possibly be adopted. For many of these animals, home is a cage, and those not adopted are often euthanized to prevent overcrowd-

---

### KNITTING FOR HOMELESS ANIMALS

• Snuggles are needed in all sizes—from fourteen inches square for cats to thirty-six inches square for large dogs. Use yarn that can be machine washed and dried, such as acrylic or cotton. (Wool collects more animal dander and dirt, and it will felt in a washing machine.)

• Visit www.h4ha.org/snuggles to find shelters that will accept your Snuggles. Or call your local animal shelter or humane society and ask them whether they accept pet blankets. Not all shelters have the washing facilities necessary to clean them.

• Feel free to donate old towels or other blankets to participating shelters as well. These castoffs easily double as Snuggles.

• For more information on Hugs for Homeless Animals and all the services they provide, contact:

Hugs for Homeless Animals
P. O. Box 320245
Franklin, WI 53132-0245
(888) 484-8180
www.h4ha.org
snuggles@h4ha.org

ing. Rae, a knitter since childhood and cofounder of the Internet list Crochet Partners, began the Snuggles Project with the most basic of creature comforts in mind—warmth and a soft place to sleep. With much help from the crocheters on her list, Rae collected, in the first year of the project, more than 200,000 Snuggles, which she sent to animal shelters nationwide. Today, blanket makers are encouraged instead to visit the Worldwide Shelter Directory on the Hugs for Homeless Animals website, and to send the blankets to a participating shelter on that list (those that accept Snuggles are marked with a kitten icon).

"We've become *the* resource for information on helping animals in shelters," says Rae, adding that theirs is the most comprehensive list of animal shelters around the world accepting volunteer help.

And animals aren't the only ones to benefit from the knitting of a Snuggle. It's an ideal first knitting project for children and other beginners. "When I teach my kids to knit," says Eric Robinson of her high school students, "I ask for something for charity in return. They are amazed that their knitting—which they think couldn't possibly be good enough—can be turned into something useful."

Finally, it's possible that Snuggles, in addition to their primary function of animal comfort, have a certain effect on pet seekers as well. "An animal is more likely to be adopted," notes Eric, "if it has a blanket in its cage." ★

> 66
> **Human Beings, indeed all sentient beings, have the right to pursue happiness and live in peace and freedom.**
> 99
>
> the XIVth DALAI LAMA

# Adopt-Me Blanket

QUITE LITERALLY, NOTHING COULD BE SIMPLER TO KNIT THAN A GARTER-STITCH SQUARE. THAT'S WHY BLANKETS FOR ANIMALS IN SHELTERS, LIKE THE ONES FEATURED HERE, ARE THE PERFECT WAY FOR BRAND-NEW KNITTERS TO BEGIN KNITTING FOR PEACE. THE GARTER STITCH ALSO CREATES A THICKER, CUSHIER BLANKET THAN OTHER KNITTING STITCHES WOULD, WHICH MEANS MORE SOFTNESS AND COMFORT IN A SHELTER PEN.

FINISHED MEASUREMENTS
To accommodate Cat (Small Dog, Medium Dog, Large Dog) 14 (18, 24, 36)" square

YARN: Approximately 200 (300, 500, 1,100) yards worsted-weight acrylic yarn
or
Approximately 150 (225, 400, 850) yards bulky-weight acrylic yarn

*Shown in Plymouth Encore (75% wool/ 25% acrylic)*

NEEDLES: One pair straight needles size US 8 (5 mm) for worsted-weight version
One pair straight needles size US 10½ (6.5 mm) for bulky-weight version
*Change needle size if necessary to obtain correct gauge.*

NOTIONS: Yarn needle

GAUGE: 18 sts = 4" (10 cm) in garter stitch, using smaller needles and worsted-weight yarn (row gauge is not crucial)
12 sts = 4" (10 cm) in garter stitch, using larger needles and bulky-weight yarn (row gauge is not crucial)

## Worsted-Weight Version
CO 63 (81, 108, 162) sts.
Work in Garter st (knit every row) until blanket measures 14 (18, 24, 36)".
BO all sts. Using yarn needle, weave in all loose ends.

## Bulky-Weight Version
CO 42 (54, 72, 108) sts.
Work in Garter st (knit every row) until blanket measures 14 (18, 24, 36)".
BO all sts. Using yarn needle, weave in all loose ends. ★

## Adopt-a-Native-Elder Program

In Native American culture, there is a tradition known as the Giveaway Circle. At its center is a custom of giving the best one has to others, be it time, skills, or possessions. Today, on Navajo reservations in northern Arizona and southern Utah, the tables are being turned. In the spirit of the Giveaway Circle, volunteers from all over the country—including knitters—are giving time, talents, and necessities like food and clothing to benefit those from whom this tradition first came.

"To offer a gift in the Native way is to give something that is of value to you," says Linda Myers of Park City, Utah, founder of the Adopt-A-Native-Elder (ANE) Program, which coordinates the giving of resources to Navajo (or Dine') elders who live traditionally on the land. "Because it is valuable, you want to share it with someone else. In this way, you honor that person with your gift."

The needs of the elders living on these reservations are great. Basic goods, such as food, warm clothing, and medical supplies are scarce; the reservations are remote; and the desert conditions are harsh. But since the late 1980s, Linda has been coordinating volunteers to donate and deliver supplies, contribute funds for food, and even knit socks.

Linda, a fiber artist, began this program after meeting a young Navajo woman in Utah who would buy food every week to send to the grandmothers and grandfathers on the reservation. "I was so moved by her devotion to the elders," she says, "that I sold a weaving I'd made and purchased $500 worth of food to bring to the elders myself." Another local weaver, Ricki Darling, heard of Linda's efforts and added her own touch: hand-knit socks to warm the elders' feet. Ricki's Knit Socks for Native Elders Program—now part of Adopt-a-Native-Elder—enlisted

> " Peace and friendship with all mankind is our wisest policy, and I wish we may be permitted to pursue it. "
>
> **THOMAS JEFFERSON**

67

> **"**
>
> **Do what you can, with what you have, where you are.**
>
> **"**
>
> THEODORE ROOSEVELT

knitters to make socks, hats, scarves, lap blankets, and children's items for elders and others living on the reservation. The Navajo sheepherders use the scarves and hats in particular.

"The elders appreciate the handwork because they are weavers themselves," says Linda, noting that the traditional lifestyle of the Navajo—the simple living conditions, the sheepherding, the weaving tradition, the Giveaway Circle—is preserved, by choice, among those on the reservation.

Helen Wojciechowski, a charity knitter in North Branford, Connecticut, embraces the idea of the Giveaway Circle with every sock she knits. "I've knit for them for years," she says of the Native elders. "You look at their photos"—printed regularly in the Adopt-a-Native-Elder newsletters volunteers receive—"and you see they're in such need. But then you look into the faces of the grandmothers and grandfathers, and you think, what *beauty*."

"They tell stories, those faces," Linda agrees, but she is most moved by something else. "Their hands are so beautiful—so soft and gnarled and gifted," she says. "Touching their hands is like touching spirit."

KNITTING FOR NATIVE ELDERS
For more information on the Adopt-a-Native-Elder Program, and to find out how you can contribute, contact:

Adopt-a-Native-Elder Program
328 W. Gregson Ave.
Salt Lake City, UT 84115
(801) 474-0535
mail@anelder.org
www.anelder.org

# Prison Knitting

IF YOU WALKED INTO DONNA BRUGGE'S CROCHETING CLASS BLINDFOLDED, YOU MIGHT EASILY MISTAKE IT FOR THE KIND THAT'S ROUTINELY HELD IN YARN SHOPS AND COMMUNITY EDUCATION CLASSROOMS. "NOW REMEMBER," SHE ANNOUNCES, "EVERYBODY'S GOING TO STITCH AT THEIR OWN TENSION," THEN LOWERS HER VOICE AS SHE GIVES SOMEONE ADVICE— "EVERY ODD ROW IS A RIGHT SIDE, SEE?"—AND SOMEONE ELSE PRAISE— "YOU SURE YOU NEVER CROCHETED BEFORE?" THE ANSWER SHE RECEIVES BEGINS TO REVEAL THE CLASS'S CONTEXT. "NO, MA'AM," A MALE VOICE DRAWLS, WITH A LAUGH. UNCOVER YOUR EYES, AND YOU'LL SEE THE SPEAKER IS A YOUNG MAN WITH A CREW CUT AND THICK FOREARMS, BLUSHING THROUGH A DEEP SUNTAN, AND CLAD IN PRISON GREENS. ⊕ Around metal tables in the cramped recreation room of

the Jackson Correctional Institution, a medium-security male prison in Black River Falls, Wisconsin, sit a dozen men dressed in identical clothing and performing similar motions. At one table, a brawny man with tattooed arms delicately loops red yarn around his pinkie and a plastic hook. Next to him sits an imposing fellow with a long ponytail and thick, furrowed eyebrows, so focused on his work he scowls. Except for recreation leader Brugge's encouragements, it's dead quiet—the concentration is almost palpable. "Damn," mutters inmate Brian Antonissen across the room, and inmate Russell Otto, whose mother taught him to crochet thirty-five years ago, comes to his rescue.

"You're doing fine," he assures him, "you've just got to relax."

"I thought this was going to be easy," Antonissen complains.

"This is rocket science, man!"

"That's the nice thing about crochet," says Otto. "If you make a mistake, you can just pull it out." His comment's double meaning is lost on no one in the room.

Men and women in prisons across the country are a mixed lot. Among them are college graduates and check forgers, schoolteachers and drug dealers, business owners and sex offenders, musicians and murderers, parents and prostitutes. Some have made a life of crime; many have simply made one bad choice. All are paying the consequences, from a few months in a county jail to life without parole in a high-security prison. But despite their diversity, they have much in common. All have done some harm to society. All have been sequestered from their families and communities in a society composed of strict rules, few privileges, and

★ ★ ★ ★ ★ ★ ★ ★ ★ ★ ★ ★

**Despite the evidence given by prisoners and those who work closely with them, it's still difficult, especially in a society that's been fed a Hollywood diet of exaggerated prison images, to imagine "hardened criminals" engaging in selfless activity, particularly one so associated with grannies in rocking chairs.**

★ ★ ★ ★ ★ ★ ★ ★ ★ ★ ★ ★

difficult personalities. All have a lot of time on their hands.

Administrators at certain prisons across the country are discovering that these two things—time and hands—can be used in a manner that benefits everyone. In these facilities, convicted criminals are taking on the gentle pursuits of knitting and crocheting. Made with donated yarn and tools, usually plastic needles and hooks that must be checked out and accounted for at all times, their finished projects are used to warm and soothe the needy in the very communities they have harmed.

The tables in the recreation room at JCI are scattered with skeins of acrylic yarn and impressive projects—from thick sweaters and hats to a child's blanket that doubles as a checkerboard, complete with checkers. Some of these projects will be given to a local charity called Project Christmas for distribution to underprivileged families in Jackson County. Others will go

to the local chapter of Project Linus (see page 82).

The inmates at JCI can knit and crochet about one hundred blankets, forty lap robes, two large boxes of scarves, and at least twenty hats and sets of mittens a year. And these types of recreational activities are not unusual. Male inmates at the Redgranite Correctional Institution in Redgranite, Wisconsin, routinely stitch and donate 150 to 200 blankets, stuffed animals, scarves, hats, and mittens a month for children's charities, including the Hands of Hope Orphanage in Botosani, Romania. Inmates at the Indiana Women's Prison in Indianapolis spin, weave, knit, and crochet items for children they have never met. Tough teenage boys at the Preston Youth Correctional Facility in Ione, California, stitch tiny togs for premature babies in the Sacramento area through Newborns in Need, and elderly folks at the VistaCare Hospice in Dallas, Texas, benefit from the talents of crocheters at the Federal Medical Center,

Carswell, in Fort Worth with each delivery of lap robes.

The image of inmates helping others may be tough to conjure. But many stereotypes of prisoners are wrong, asserts Captain Julia Dunaway, chief social worker at Carswell. "You don't think people in prison will care about the welfare of someone else," she says, "but give them the opportunity, and you'll be amazed at what they'll do."

"It feels good to give something to kids who are needy," says JCI inmate Remijio Sanchez. "My family were migrant workers. I know what it's like to go without."

"I grew up on welfare and didn't have much as a kid," Brian Antonissen adds, looking up from the pink-and-blue scarf he's struggling over. "If I do this, maybe someone else won't have to freeze this winter."

Instilling a desire to give something back to the community that one has harmed is perhaps the number one reason that knitting and crocheting programs exist in prisons today. "We call it 'restorative justice,'" says Sandy Hand, a recreation therapist at the Minnesota Correctional Facility–Shakopee, which houses women offenders at all levels of security. "The principle behind it is that crime affects everyone in a community, not just the victim. Our program helps them deal with their crimes and contribute to the community they've hurt."

In other facilities, similar programs are required by the prisoner's sentence, but with additional outcomes in mind. At Limon Correctional Facility, which houses the toughest male prison population in Colorado, crocheting, machine knitting, and quilting are a part of Therapeutic Community, a court-mandated program designed to help inmates develop anger management skills, patience, and other social skills as they create stuffed animals that local police give to children in traumatic situations.

"It *is* rehabilitative," says John Martin, an inmate at JCI. "It makes

★ ★ ★ ★ ★ ★ ★ ★ ★ ★ ★ ★ ★

**"These are no-nonsense, hardened guys," says Skip LaBarge of the inmates he supervises in Therapeutic Community at Limon Correctional Facility in Colorado, where male offenders, some built like trucks with tattoos over 90 percent of their bodies, are serving ten years to multiple life sentences under maximum security. Still, they possess remarkable ingenuity; the animals they machine-knit and crochet, like the items inmates in most prisons create, are not made from patterns, but through canny thinking. "You ain't seen nothin'," LaBarge says, "until a guy doing 800 years comes up to you all proud and bustin' because he just crocheted his first cow."**

★ ★ ★ ★ ★ ★ ★ ★ ★ ★ ★ ★

My cellmate called me an old lady," says Adam Caraballo of JCI, "but after watching me for four hours, he asked me to teach him, too." "I'm looking forward to putting a lot of smiles on parents and kids," says inmate Juan Guzman. "It's good to have a gift and share it."

you use your head, and it relaxes you." Seated beside him, Adam Caraballo breaks his concentration to grumble, "I don't have much patience." Does crocheting help? "I hope so," he says.

Other benefits of the knitting and crocheting programs run deeper, and may be harder to see if you're not directly involved with the inmates. "It's turned these girls' lives around," says Jackie Merriman, who distributes yarn to the Carswell facility in Fort Worth. "For the first time in their lives, they can point to something and say, 'I did this—I'm giving something back to the community.'"

"Many women here have never accomplished a lot," says Sandy Hand of the inmates at Shakopee in Minnesota. "Now, they can experience pride and joy. Imperfection doesn't matter. There's such a sense of accomplishment simply in completing something."

While there's no hard evidence to prove that knitting alone can convert criminals into law-abiding, community-serving

citizens, handcraft programs like these do make an impact, both inside and outside prison walls. "The people in these knitting classes will be back in our neighborhoods in a short time," says Bernie Sullivan, public information officer for the Bristol County sheriff's office, in defense of the knitting program at the Dartmouth House of Corrections, a women's facility in Dartmouth, Massachusetts. "What they will need most is a sense of self-worth. We're trying to help them believe in themselves, learn some skills, and pick up their responsibilities."

"The biggest thing these guys learn is how to interact with each other, respecting each other's qualities and uniqueness," says Ron Holmes, recreation leader at Redgranite in Wisconsin. "It also gives them a taste of 'normal' life; they talk about daily events, get a little bit of freedom, build camaraderie."

"It's a peaceful time to get away," adds Sandy Hand, "to talk about your kids instead of institution stuff, to just socialize." Here is a chance for inmates to gather in quiet company, remember that they are humans and members of families, laugh and tell stories, and reflect on mistakes they've made.

"One of the most important things we do is listen," says Jean Cleavinger, who teaches knitting at the Boulder County Jail in Boulder, Colorado. "We listen to their problems and their thoughts about what to do differently when they get out. We help them think through ways they can stay out of jail, or deal with abusive relationships and alcoholics in their families. We encourage them, telling them they're good people who've made mistakes and letting them know that someone believes in them."

Says Carswell's Julia Dunaway, "I think it even surprises the prisoners. When they're given something positive to do, they fall in love with the feeling they get from helping others."

"Other inmates tease you," admits JCI's Jeffrey Noggle, "but once you make something, they get interested, and once they learn it's for children who don't have warm stuff to wear, it's all okay."

The generosity of prison handcrafters makes a difference in other ways as well. The more goods local charities receive from them, the more society's perceptions of these men and women behind bars begin to shift. "When we first started this program," says Redgranite's Ron Holmes, "there were charities that wouldn't accept our donations because they were made by prisoners. But when they saw who *was* accepting these donations, and what beautiful things they got, they changed their minds. As one of our inmates likes to say, not everyone here is a thug."

"People think of us as monsters," says JCI inmate Jose Ortiz, "but I know I'm a good person. Giving to others helps lift that image."

"All we did on the outside was drink, do crime," adds Guzman, "but this shows people we're willing to change."

And the volunteers who keep the knitting programs going are helping to dispel the prisoners' misconceptions about people on the outside. "It means so much to these women to know there are people in the 'real world' who care about them," says Terrie Sigler of her volunteer work with the knitters at the Indiana Women's Prison. "It means so much to know people will act consistently, live up to their word, and show up when they say they will. In turn, these women share with me everything they have— their attention, their hugs, their love, their lives."

Back at the Jackson Correctional Institution, the inmates are considering some of the other benefits of knitting and crocheting as they count chain stitches and ply their plastic hooks. "It does make the time go by," David Austin points out.

"And we," adds Russell Otto, "have nothing but time." ★

# Knitting for Cancer Causes

GRACEFUL STITCHES IS A UNIQUE KIND OF YARN STORE. WALK IN, AND YOU'LL SEE A VERY PRETTY SCENE. A DELICIOUS ASSORTMENT OF YARNS FILLS THE SHELVES, RANGING FROM FUN NOVELTIES TO RICH CASHMERES TO CLASSIC WOOLS. FLOWERS ARE ARRANGED IN BUNCHES, AND WOMEN ARE GATHERED TOO, SELECTING YARNS, SHARING STORIES, AND, OF COURSE, KNITTING. ⊕ This may not sound so different from other upscale yarn stores you have seen, but Graceful Stitches is one of a kind. Located in Medfield, Massachusetts, the shop is run completely by volunteers, and 100 percent of its profits are donated to cancer research or other cancer causes. Nearly all of the women knitting here have been touched by cancer too. And considering that, according to American Cancer Society statistics, more than 200,000 women are diagnosed with breast cancer every year and more than 76,000 with other gynecologic cancers, it's no surprise. Many of the store's volunteers and customers have some form of cancer themselves, and are finding the process of knitting soothing and the supportive atmosphere of the shop an oasis in a life filled with chemotherapy, radiation, and uncertainty. Other women at Graceful Stitches love someone with cancer—a husband, a child, a parent, a friend. Still others are here simply because they love to knit, and are glad their passion can help ease someone's suffering.

While the idea of a yarn store completely devoted to cancer knitting may be something new, it is, in reality, one of many creative uses of knitting to raise awareness of cancer, support cancer research, and supply cancer patients with knitted items meant to bestow comfort, love, and peace. The word *knitting* is often synonymous with *healing*—broken bones knit themselves together, as do broken societies and broken hearts. For many with cancer, no matter what kind, this connection is particularly real.

Graceful Stitches is the outgrowth of a long-lasting friendship between two women, Karen Bailey and Carol Venie. Best friends since high school—when they used to knit together—the women lost touch in adulthood, but rekindled their friendship when they discovered a common plight: Karen had developed colon cancer, and Carol breast cancer. Bonded by this coincidence of misfortune, Karen and Carol quickly fell back into their high school habits of talking, laughing, crying, and knitting together.

The year was 2001, at the

height of the novelty-yarn scarf craze, and scarves were what they were knitting. When a neighbor invited them to sell their handknit scarves as part of a Christmas boutique she was hosting in her home, Carol and Karen agreed, on one condition: that the money from the sale of their scarves would be donated to cancer research. "Then other people started asking, 'Can you bring scarves to a party at my house?'" Karen says, and Graceful Stitches was born.

Seeing the home party format as a way their knitting could benefit others who, like themselves, had been affected by cancer (both women today have clean bills of

health), the friends began knitting scarves and coordinating parties. In no time, their fund-raising scarf parties became enormously popular. Karen and Carol began recruiting volunteer knitters, many of whom were affected by cancer in some way themselves, and all of whom were eager to help. "We made $60,000 that first year," Karen recalls, an incredible feat considering that they were buying yarn off the shelf, at least at first, and using Karen's living room for storage.

Now, with nonprofit status and a spacious storefront location, Graceful Stitches has evolved into a gathering place as well as a yarn store where customers can purchase yarn, knitting supplies, and knitted scarves.

The profits from store sales go to cancer hospitals and research facilities in the Boston area. Proceeds from home party sales benefit a cancer cause of the party hostess's choice—say, the study of the neuroblastoma her child has been diagnosed with, or assistance

VOLUNTEERING AT GRACEFUL STITCHES
For more information on Graceful Stitches, including how you can volunteer, visit www.graceful stitches.org, call (508) 359-1505, or visit the retail shop at:

Graceful Stitches
505 Main Street
Medfield, MA 02052

★ ★ ★ ★ ★ ★ ★ ★ ★ ★ ★ ★

Knitting to help others soothes one's own pain, and knowing that others are seeking peace through similar means—that you are not alone in your experience—is priceless. Karen Bailey has another word for it, reflected in the very name *Graceful Stitches*. "I feel that with God's grace, Carol and I survived cancer," she says. "Everything about this endeavor is graceful: The scarves are graceful, the women are graceful." And having a way to share your burdens and worries with others, having a place where you can be heard and understood—that, too, is grace.

★ ★ ★ ★ ★ ★ ★ ★ ★ ★ ★ ★

for a family struggling to pay medical bills. In its short lifespan, says Karen, Graceful Stitches has raised more than $100,000 toward cancer causes. Best of all, however, may be the sisterhood and the spirit and the devotion that has blossomed within the shop and among the volunteers, wherever they may be. One shop volunteer recently suffered a relapse of her colon cancer. "But I'll be back once I know my chemo schedule," she said.

The idea of knitting indulgent, beautiful scarves to benefit cancer research is one that occurred to another woman at about the same time it occurred to Karen Bailey and Carol Venie of Graceful Stitches. But Marta McGinnis, the founder of Knit for Her Cure and a

SUPPORT KNIT FOR HER CURE
To learn more about Knit for Her Cure, or to purchase a scarf kit from the online boutique, visit www.knitforhercure.com, e-mail info@knitforhercure.com, or call (916) 630-1201.

former cancer patient herself, approached it from a slightly different angle. Marta could attest to the powerfully soothing qualities of knitting, but she also saw a practical need to fill. "It's freezing cold in chemotherapy treatment centers," she says, recalling the hours she sat waiting for treatment with other women, who were often alone. "There are hospital blankets, but they don't offer much comfort."

Marta's plan was to give scarves—as soft and full of sentiment as a "big warm hug"—to women in chemotherapy treatment centers, many of whom have uterine or ovarian cancer, "I've known about breast cancer, supported its research, written about it for years," says Marta, a marketing professional with a long history of promoting women's events. "This one"—gynecologic cancer—"needed more attention."

With yarn supplied by Muench Yarns of Petaluma, California (whose owner, Kristin Muench, lost her mother to ovarian cancer), and with patterns

contributed by such designers as Sally Melville, Nicky Epstein, and Suss Cousins, Marta created eight different scarf kits that could be marketed to yarn stores nationwide, with a portion of proceeds going to the Chicago-based Gynecologic Cancer Foundation. She launched her idea in 2003 at Big Sky Studio (now Big Sky Luxury Yarns), the Lafayette, California, shop where her knitting group met. "It was phenomenally successful," she reports. "We had all kinds of knitters—young girls on up—from all over the Bay Area." That day, 600 kits were sold and 400 scarves completed.

To date, more than 3,500 Knit for Her Cure kits have been sold through participating yarn stores. The resulting scarves may be kept and worn by the knitter, given to a friend who has cancer, or given back to the shop from which the kit was bought, to be given to a woman undergoing chemotherapy at a local treatment center. The comfort provided by these scarves is far more than physical. "It's so

**KNITTING FOR CHEMOCAPS**
For hat patterns and further information on ChemoCaps, visit www.chemocaps.com.

important for these women to know someone cares about them, even a stranger," says Marta.

JoAnne Turcotte would second that motion. As a longtime charity knitter and the designer of the hat on page 78, she too has close connections with cancer and cancer knitting. She originally designed the hat—and several others—for ChemoCaps.com, an organization that distributes warm, soft handknit hats to chemotherapy patients, thus "comforting their heads and their souls."

ChemoCaps.com was founded by Ronni Spoll and her daughter, Heather. The two frequently knit at Kraemer Yarn Shop in Nazareth, Pennsylvania, where JoAnne worked and taught. Heather, an art teacher and avid knitter, was undergoing chemotherapy at the time, and saw knitting caps as a

way to comfort others enduring the same treatment. In 2000, Heather passed away at age twenty-five.

ChemoCaps.com—also known as the "Heather Spoll No Hair Day Hat Program"—was born out of Ronni's desire to extend the comfort and sense of caring a handknit ChemoCap could provide to cancer patients. "I saw this as a way to turn the negative into a positive," says Ronni, and she has succeeded in doing so. Since the program began, knitters in the United States and worldwide have participated by knitting and donating ChemoCaps to cancer treatment centers in their communities, an act of generosity that Ronni wishes to encourage and applaud. "On behalf of every cancer patient who is a recipient of a handknit ChemoCap, I thank them," she says. ★

" Better than a thousand hollow words is one word that brings peace. "

BUDDHA

# ChemoCaps Eyelet Hat

## —DESIGNED BY JOANNE TURCOTTE—

BE SURE TO MAKE THIS ELEGANT HAT OUT OF A VERY SOFT, WARM, EASY-CARE YARN. COTTON AND COTTON BLENDS WORK WELL, AND VERY SOFT ANIMAL FIBERS—LIKE MERINO WOOL AND ALPACA—MAY ALSO BE APPRECIATED. IF YOU KNOW HER, CHECK WITH THE RECIPIENT BEFORE YOU START TO FIND OUT IF HER SKIN IS SENSITIVE TO ANY FIBERS.

FINISHED MEASUREMENTS
Small (Medium, Large)
Finished hat circumference:
17½ (19, 20¼)"

YARN: Approximately 200 yards sport-weight yarn

*Samples shown in GGH Maxima (100% merino superwash)*

NEEDLES: 1 set of double-pointed needles (dpn) size US 5 (3.75 mm)
One 16" circular (circ) needle size US 5 (optional)
*Change needle size if necessary to obtain correct gauge.*

NOTIONS: Stitch markers, yarn needle

GAUGE: 22 sts and 28 rnds = 4" in Stockinette stitch (St st)

## Eyelet Pattern

(multiple of 8 sts)
Rnd 1: K5, *k2tog, yo, k6, repeat from * to last 3 sts, k2tog, yo, k1.
Rnd 2: Knit.
Rnd 3: K4, *k2tog, yo, k2tog, yo, k4, repeat from * to last 4 sts, k2tog, yo, k2tog, yo.
Rnds 4-8: Knit.
Rnd 9: K1, *k2tog, yo, k6, repeat from * to last 7 stitches, k2tog, yo, k5.
Rnd 10: Knit.
Rnd 11: *K2tog, yo, k2tog, yo, k4, repeat from * to end.
Rnds 12-16: Knit.

## Hat

CO 96 (104, 112) sts. Distribute sts evenly on three needles, or use a circ needle. Join for working in the rnd, being careful not to twist sts; place marker (pm) for beginning of rnd.

Begin in St st; work 12 (12, 14) rnds even. Change to Eyelet Pattern; work even until hat measures 6 (6½, 7)" from cast-on edge, ending by working a knit rnd other than Rnd 2 or Rnd 10.

On the next rnd, decrease as follows, beginning with decrease rnd 3 (2, 1).
*Note: If you are using a circ needle, change to dpn when necessary for number of sts remaining.*

Rnd 1: *K12, k2tog, repeat from * around. [Size Large—104 sts remain.]
Rnd 2: *K11, k2tog, repeat from * around. [Sizes Medium and Large—96 sts remain.]
Rnd 3: *K10, k2tog, repeat from * around—88 sts remain.
Rnd 4: *K9, k2tog, repeat from * around—80 sts remain.
Rnd 5: *K8, k2tog, repeat from * around—72 sts remain.
Rnd 6: *K7, k2tog, repeat from * around—64 sts remain.
Rnd 7: *K6, k2tog, repeat from * around—56 sts remain.
Rnd 8: *K5, k2tog, repeat from * around—48 sts remain.
Rnd 9: *K4, k2tog, repeat from * around—40 sts remain.
Rnd 10: *K3, k2tog, repeat from * around—32 sts remain.
Rnd 11: *K2, k2tog, repeat from * around—24 sts remain.
Rnd 12: *K1, k2tog, repeat from * around—16 sts remain.
Rnd 13: *K2tog, repeat from * around—8 sts remain.

## Finishing

Cut yarn, leaving a 12" tail. Thread yarn through remaining sts, then draw tight and fasten off securely. Using yarn needle, weave in all loose ends. ★

# Peace
—FOR—
## Kids

# Project Linus

MUCH IS MADE THESE DAYS OF HOMELAND SECURITY, AN EFFORT TO PROTECT THE BORDERS OF THE UNITED STATES, KEEP WARY EYES OPEN TO SUSPICIOUS ACTIVITY, AND GENERALLY GUARD OURSELVES FROM THOSE WHO MIGHT HURT US. BUT TAKE A PEEK UNDER THE COVERS OF OVERT SECURITY MEASURES IN OUR COUNTRY, PEEL BACK THE LAYERS OF EVERYDAY AMERICAN ACTIVITY, AND YOU'LL FIND AN EXTRAORDINARY GROUP OF KNITTERS AND OTHER CRAFTERS BUSILY WORKING TOWARD SECURITY OF ANOTHER KIND—A SECURITY OF THE HEART. ⊕ All are invited to participate, no matter their background or demographic, and all are helped, regardless of circumstance. It's an effort born of opening up to others with love, not closing off from fear. Is it effective? Just ask the children, families, and crafters involved in

Project Linus, a nationwide effort to bring peace, comfort, and love to critically ill and traumatized children in the form of handmade security blankets.

"A Project Linus blanket is like a portable hug," says Karen Loucks, Project Linus's founder, and her words hark back to a time when, for many of us, life seemed less complicated and solace could be found in a tattered, beloved blanket. Today, national security threats aside, many children and their families live lives marked by terrors of all kinds—cancer or other illnesses, school shootings, and natural disasters. It doesn't seem like a blanket could mean much in the face of such illness or violence, but, surprisingly, it does.

Project Linus began on Christmas Eve in 1995, when Karen, a thirty-four-year-old knitter from Denver, Colorado, read an article

in *Parade* magazine in which a three-year-old girl, undergoing chemotherapy for leukemia, looked to a special blanket as a source of comfort and security. Karen, who had worked on a fund-raiser for the Rocky Mountain Cancer Center in Denver, realized she could use her love of yarn arts to benefit sick children in a very tangible way. By collecting knitted, crocheted, and quilted children's blankets from area crafters recruited through a newspaper article, she began literally blanketing the cancer center—and the sick kids there—with love and care.

With the blessing of Charles Schultz, Karen named her project after the Peanuts character Linus, who best illustrates what the organization is all about, because he is never separated from his own security blanket. Project Linus spread throughout the country as crafters formed local area chapters in response to the needs of children in hospitals and shelters in their own communities, resulting in a nationwide network of "blanketeers."

Since its founding, over one million blankets have been donated through Project Linus. Better put, that's over one million seriously ill or traumatized kids who, with their families, have received some peace from the generous hands and hearts of strangers. Project Linus has grown tremendously since its inception— as chapter coordinators who have weathered its growing pains will tell you—and today, behind the stacks of soft, colorful blankets making their way to children in hospitals, schools, and shelters is a rock-solid organization of deeply committed volunteers.

Karen Loucks now serves Project Linus as the chapter coordinator of the Denver area, where she works as an emergency medical technician for the Children's Hospital. In this position, she has the honor of delivering blankets to the children admitted there every day. "I set up their rooms when they first come in," she says, "and I always lay a Project Linus blanket across their bed. For a kid who is really sick, the objects close by you—like your pillow, like your blanket—become really important."

"We always say that a Project Linus blanket is like a special kind of medicine," says Mary Balagna, the vice president of Project Linus. "When you put that blanket around a child's shoulders, it gives them a hug of comfort that medicine just can't. We've had abuse counselors tell us that children will wrap a blanket around their shoulders or over their head, and then they'll be able to talk—it's almost like a shield of protection. Children who have to undergo tests calm down when the blanket is wrapped around them. Or they'll take the blanket into surgery with them, or hold it through a terrible circumstance, and they won't put it down for weeks."

★ ★ ★ ★ ★ ★ ★ ★ ★ ★ ★ ★

At any given time, about 350 chapters of Project Linus are operating in the United States, usually with at least one chapter in each state. This ensures not only that blankets are created, collected, and distributed within each locale, but also that, in the case of an emergency somewhere in the nation, reserves of blankets can be called up from chapters across the country and sent exactly where they need to be, within hours.

★ ★ ★ ★ ★ ★ ★ ★ ★ ★ ★

The blankets donated to Project Linus are as diverse as the handcrafters who make them and the children who receive them. They range from tiny knitted baby blankets that wrap premature babies in neonatal intensive-care units to sturdy toddler-size quilts to couch-size crocheted afghans for teenagers.

★ ★ ★ ★ ★ ★ ★ ★ ★ ★ ★

> ❝
> **Knit on,
> with
> confidence
> and hope,
> through all
> crises.**
> ❞
>
> ELIZABETH ZIMMERMANN

"We don't ever kid ourselves into thinking that we're curing cancer or putting children back with their families," adds Project Linus president Carol Babbitt. "But I also think you can't discount the difference that this makes to somebody—because it's handmade, because it's a blanket, which means comfort."

Carol and Mary, both of central Illinois, have run Project Linus since 2000, and under their direction the organization has blossomed into something Karen Loucks never dreamed it could be. For both Carol and Mary, Project Linus is a full-time-plus volunteer operation. "We live for Project Linus," Carol says. Together, they set clear rules for chapter coordinators, keep operations consistent and unified, and ensure the Project Linus network runs as smoothly as possible.

This network was given its first big test in 1999, with a tragedy that struck close to Karen's home: the Columbine school shooting in Littleton, Colorado. "On the day the shooting happened," Carol recalls, "Karen and some others gathered up all the blankets they had on hand and took them to a church in the area where kids were being sent for counseling. Karen told a secretary in the church, 'I'm from Project Linus. I've got these blankets, and I think they might help.' The secretary said, 'Really, I don't think they will. These are older kids, and I can't see how blankets will make a difference.'" Karen politely offered to leave them in a corner of the room where the students were gathering, just in case, and she left. The next time the church secretary passed that room, she found the students sitting in a circle, every one of them with a blanket wrapped around their shoulders. "They were talking," Carol says, "and they were crying. The secretary called Karen back and said, 'I need all the blankets you can get me, *now.*'"

As word spread through the Project Linus network, coordinators sent hundreds of blankets to Karen, who ensured that every Columbine student who wanted a blanket—more than 1,600, all told—received one. The tragedy was a good drill for future events; after September 11, 2001, Project Linus sent more than 10,000 blankets to New York City and 600 to the Pentagon in two weeks' time.

That event also spawned Project Linus's annual Make a Blanket Day, essentially a blanket-making marathon that takes place in shopping malls, churches, and schools the third Saturday of February. Each chapter hosts its own event, an opportunity to gather volunteers for a day of camaraderie and crafting, and an effort to bolster each chapter's supply for the year. Nationwide, the day garners about 100,000 blankets.

The volunteers who gather at Make a Blanket Days, as well as those who knit, crochet, and quilt in schools, Scout groups, assisted-living facilities, or the quiet of their own homes, are "a special breed of people," as Mary says, "people who have kind, generous hearts and will do whatever they can to help.

They come together truly from all walks of life," she adds. "It's important to open our doors to all.

"People are more than happy to donate anonymously a work of art that they've created to whoever needs it," continues Mary. "And it doesn't matter what that child's circumstances are. Donors don't care who the recipients are or where they come from, what kind of family they have, or what has happened to them—they're just happy to bring them peace, bring them comfort." ★

KNITTING FOR PROJECT LINUS
• Blankets are welcome in all sizes, as kids of all sizes need them. The greatest need is for teenagers, who require larger blankets in less juvenile colors. Project Linus labels will be sewn onto the blankets upon receipt by the chapter coordinator.

• Use yarn that can be machine washed and dried, such as acrylic or cotton. Note that these blankets are intended to provide comfort more than warmth.

• Visit www.projectlinus.org to find the chapter nearest you, and send your completed blankets to the chapter coordinator listed there. If no chapter is local to you, consider donating blankets to local hospitals, homeless shelters, women's shelters, and more.

• For more information, contact:

Project Linus National Headquarters
P.O. Box 5621
Bloomington, IL 61702-5621
(309) 664-7814
www.projectlinus.org
information@projectlinus.org

# Project Linus Security Blanket

A SOFT, EVER-PRESENT BLANKET LENDS PEACE TO KIDS OF ALL AGES IN STRESSFUL SITUATIONS. THE SMALLER SECURITY BLANKET SHOWN HERE IS PERFECT FOR A YOUNG CHILD OR BABY; THE LARGER SIZE WILL COMFORT A TEEN.

KNIT IN A MODIFIED FAN-AND-FEATHER STITCH, THIS BLANKET IS PRETTY AND EXTREMELY EASY TO COMPLETE—THE ENTIRE PATTERN CONSISTS OF THREE ROWS, TWO OF WHICH INVOLVE STRAIGHT KNITTING OR PURLING. THESE BLANKETS ARE WELL-LOVED AND WELL-USED BY KIDS, SO BE SURE TO CHOOSE A WASHABLE YARN. IF YOU'RE UNSURE ABOUT A YARN'S WASHABILITY, KNIT A SWATCH, THEN RUN IT THROUGH THE WASHER AND DRYER TO SEE IF IT WILL WORK.

FINISHED MEASUREMENTS
Approximately 36 (48)" square

YARN: Approximately 875 (1450) yards washable worsted-weight yarn

*Sample shown in Brown Sheep Company Cotton Fleece (80% cotton/20% merino wool)*

NEEDLES: One 24" circular (circ) needle size US 9 (5.5 mm) for light worsted-weight yarn or
One 24" circular (circ) needle size US 10 (6 mm) for medium to heavy worsted-weight yarn
*Change needle size if necessary to obtain correct gauge.*

NOTIONS: Yarn needle

GAUGE: 16 sts and 30 rows = 4" (10 cm) in blanket pattern stitch

## Blanket

CO 144 (210) sts.
Row 1: K1, *yo, k3, [k2tog] twice, k3, yo, k1. Repeat from * across.
Row 2: Purl.
Row 3: Knit.
Repeat Rows 1–3 until blanket measures 36 (48)" from beginning. BO all sts. ★

# Binky Patrol

If Project Linus's key to success is being a well-oiled machine, the secret of Binky Patrol, another organization that distributes handmade blankets—in this case, Binkies—to children, is a core group of people with uniquely complementary talents. From the knitters and sewers who create the Binkies, to the marketing and legal professionals who donate their time and skills, to founder Susan Finch, a website designer, there's a volunteer to meet every need of Binky Patrol. "It's a lot of quiet giving," says Susan of the talents that combine to make sure kids across the nation get comfort and peace in trying times.

The word *Binky* (etymology: *blanket* to *blankie* to *Binky*) is a lighthearted term describing any object that brings a child comfort. "Binkies help kids know they're not forgotten," says Susan, "that somebody's thinking about them all the time, whether we know them or not." The kids who receive Binkies run the gamut, from kids with AIDS and kids with cancer to homeless kids and kids in juvenile detention centers. "I couldn't care less who gets a blanket," says Susan. "I don't care what their background is. They're children—you don't judge them. In my mind, all kids are the same. If they need a Binky, they get one."

Susan began Binky Patrol in 1996 while running a struggling art gallery in Laguna Beach, California. Her mother, Josephine Roush, asked if she would help sew blankets for unwed mothers at a nearby shelter. As Susan did, "a lightbulb went on for me," she says. "I thought, I bet there are a lot of people like me that want to help an organization, but who need to do it on their own time, at home, like independent study. So I drew up a little logo, came up with a name, and four hours later, an organization was born." After an early mention on the *Oprah Winfrey Show*, Susan's tiny organization went nationwide within thirty days. "I didn't even have nonprofit status yet," she said, "but I had a friend who does this kind of thing for a living set up a corporation fast, and local clothing manufacturers sent tons of spare fabric. I let the gallery go and got a job at a public relations firm. They took Binky Patrol on as a pro bono project. Everybody helped with what they already did."

As word spread, chapters were set up across the country. Since its rocket-propelled start, Binky Patrol has given out about 300,000 knit, crocheted, and sewn blankets to kids who need the kind of solace only a Binky can bring.

Binky Patrol's publicity director, Carolyn Berndt, has seen the power of a Binky firsthand. A former marketing professional, Carolyn now spends her days raising two children, writing press releases and giving talks about Binky Patrol, and distributing Binkies near her home in Orange County, California. "Most of the time, I deliver them to the administrative staff of hospitals, shelters, or foster care agencies," she says. "But occasionally, I get to give them directly to kids, and boy, does that suck you in quickly. Once I brought them to a group home for boys aged eight to fifteen. At first it was like 'yeah, whatever'—typical teenage boy behavior. Within ten minutes, they were all sitting around the TV in the family room, watching football, and every single one of them was curled up in his Binky." Susan argues that teenagers have the greatest need for Binkies. "They're older," she says, "they've seen more hurt and pain. They're also forgotten more."

Still, even the smallest children need Binkies to get them started in life. "We hear from parents of babies in intensive care," says Carolyn, "who have been so stressed and so sad because their baby was born prematurely. They walk into the NICU (neonatal intensive care unit), and every baby there has a Binky. It brings so much color to the NICU; it makes them feel so happy."

Binky Patrol's blanketeers include Girl Scouts who churn out hundreds during annual Bink-A-Thons, two elderly women who make a Binky a day each, and the volunteers who coordinate the 110-odd chapters in about forty states. "People volunteer for a variety of reasons," says Susan. "Sometimes it's because they want to help; sometimes it's because they're filling up a hole in their own lives. Many are gaining valuable skills from Binky Patrol: leadership, public relations, organization, website creation. They end up with job skills—and confidence."

As long as there are sad, scared, or hurt children in the country, there will be plenty of need for handmade touchstones of comfort—whether Binkies or security blankets. Neither Project Linus nor Binky Patrol sees the other as competition. "It's just more kids getting blankets," says Susan. "I wish we'd run out of children to give them to. Wouldn't that be a wonderful world?"

---

**KNITTING FOR BINKY PATROL**

• Binky Patrol blankets should be no smaller than 36 inches square—the largest are about the size of a twin bed cover. Again, the greatest need is for teenagers, so larger sizes in more mature colors are especially welcome. Once received, each blanket will have a Binky Patrol label sewn in a corner.

• Blankets must be machine washable, so choose yarn accordingly. Consider acrylics, cottons, washable wools, and blends.

• Visit www.binkypatrol.org for a list of local chapters, and send completed blankets to the one nearest you. Alternatively, send them to a local hospital or facility that serves children in need, or send them to:

Binky Patrol, Inc.
c/o Carolyn Berndt
19065 Ridgeview Road
Villa Park, CA 92861

• For more information, contact:

Binky Patrol, Inc.
P.O. Box 1468
Laguna Beach, CA 92652-1468
(949) 916-5926
www.binkypatrol.org
binky@binkypatrol.org

# Care Wear Volunteers

MANY KNITTERS' FIRST CHARITY ITEM IS A SMALL ONE: A SCARF, MAYBE A PAIR OF SOCKS OR MITTENS. IT'S SURPRISING, THEN, WHEN THE PIECES GET EVEN SMALLER, AND YOU FIND YOURSELF KNITTING A HAT THAT COULD FIT AN ORANGE—BUT INSTEAD IT'S FOR A TINY BABY. BONNIE HAGERMAN, FOUNDER OF CARE WEAR VOLUNTEERS, HAS INSPIRED MANY A KNITTER TO TRY HER HAND AT SUCH LILLIPUTIAN PROPORTIONS. ☮ Bonnie speaks in an articulate, crisp manner, yet her voice is also warm, with a current of mirth bubbling beneath it. The qualities suggested by her voice—well-organized and matter-of-fact, yet pleasant and genuinely caring—are prerequisites for her dual roles, both of which she performs from her office at Hood College, a small liberal arts school in Frederick, Maryland. Bonnie is the executive director of academic and career services at Hood; in this role she assigns advisers to new students, oversees a number of student-support offices, and generally helps ease students' transitions into college. She is also the coordinator of Care Wear Volunteers, a nationwide knitting effort to clothe premature babies in neonatal intensive care units with mittens, booties, and, of course, hats.

It doesn't take long to knit a preemie hat, and the rewards are significant for all involved. For the knitter, there's the nearly instant gratification of finishing an item and the vision of that hat fitting snugly on the head of a tiny infant. The preemie's benefits are more physical; the hats help retain body heat, relieving stress on the baby's circulatory system, which doesn't have to work as hard to keep the body warm.

The colorful handmade hats also soften the preemie's sterile environment and call attention away from the abundant tubes, ventilators, and monitors, helping the preemie look a little bit more like a normal, healthy baby. This effect also brings a certain psychological comfort to the baby's parents. The hats are a tender expression of human kindness at a critical time and, regardless of the outcome, they become a precious memento of the baby's first days in this world. One hat, though small enough to cup in your hand, is a potent symbol of love and dedication and, above all, hope.

"With hats is how we began," says Bonnie of Care Wear, which she started in 1991 after reading a magazine article about a group in Ohio that was knitting hats and sewing kimono-style gowns for preemies in a local hospital. An avid knitter and sewer with experience teaching textiles classes at Hood, Bonnie saw this as a community service need she could help fill and obtained the names of ten hospitals in her Mid-Atlantic area in need of help. She set her sights on Children's National Medical Center in nearby Washington, D.C., and began knitting hats. "Back in 1990, this was a need that wasn't being addressed," Bonnie recalls, "and there were no patterns." Scaling down a hat pattern for full-term infants, she started knitting samples in a size she could only guess preemies would wear. The staff at Children's said they would love them, but she'd have to make them smaller.

"I went back to the knitting needles," says Bonnie, "sent a couple more samples, and got another call. The hospital employee said, 'Perfect! But you have to make them smaller.' I think it was on the third try that the employee said to me in desperation, 'Please, go to the grocery store and buy a lime. Make a hat to fit a head the size of a lime.'" The elongated shape was a more accurate representation of a preemie's head, and yes, the smallest were that small.

"I was thinking I could make

KNITTING FOR CARE WEAR
• Visit www.carewear.org to view a database of hospitals near you that accept knitted donations (or see "Knitting for Babies Near You" on page 93).

• Preemie knits must be very soft and washable in hot water, harsh detergents, and disinfectants. Use soft acrylic, cotton, or cotton/acrylic yarns. Some infants are sensitive to wool.

• Generally, hospitals need hats to fit the heads of preemies as well as full-term infants, since preemies aren't the only babies in NICUs.

• Check with your hospital liaison before attaching decorations such as pompoms, bows, or other possibly detachable trims. While they generally are not dangerous (preemies aren't very mobile, and risk of the trim becoming a choking hazard is low), some hospitals forbid them. If they are allowed, be sure to attach them very securely.

• Place finished items in plastic bags to keep them clean. Do not add potpourri, sachets, or fragrances, and don't use fabric softeners if you wash the items before sending them. (They will be washed and sterilized at the hospital upon receipt, so washing is generally not necessary.) It's essential that items knit for preemies be free of cigarette smoke odors.

• Hospitals that accept knitted neonatal items are often overwhelmed with tiny hats. Check with your hospital liaison to identify specific needs, and consider making blankets, booties, or other items if hats are overabundant (www.carewear.org offers a wide variety of patterns).

• For more information, contact:

Care Wear Volunteers, Inc.
Bonnie Hagerman
c/o Hood College
401 Rosemont Avenue
Frederick, MD 21701
(301) 696-3550
www.carewear.org
hagerman@hood.edu

thirty hats a month, and I came up with patterns in a range of sizes," she says, noting that NICUs need hats in sizes fitting preemies to full-term infants. "I asked how many they'd need at Children's—I didn't want to overwhelm them—and they said they could use between 75 and 125 hats a month, and, by the way, could I make booties and mittens to go with them?" Her voice takes on that bubbling undercurrent of amusement: "It was then I realized that my knitting skills were not up to this task," she says, and she set about recruiting other knitters. "I figured that if this tugged at my heartstrings," she says, "it certainly would tug at other people's."

She called her local newspaper, the *Frederick News Post*, which ran a feature on Care Wear. Bonnie received responses from 150 people, and she sent photocopies of her patterns to all of them. Knitted, crocheted, and sewn items began to pour in regularly, and Bonnie acted as Care Wear Central, collecting items and

forwarding them to the NICUs on her list. A few years later, after receiving publicity in the *Washington Post* and *Family Circle*, and after expanding Care Wear's contributions to a greater number of hospitals, Bonnie found herself so overwhelmed with tiny knitted items that she had to relinquish her post as collector and distributor, instead encouraging volunteers to donate items to hospitals in their own communities.

How many items are knit through Care Wear today? "I haven't a clue," Bonnie laughs. "I stopped counting when I stopped collecting. At that time, it was about 28,000—that was almost ten years ago."

Today, she measures Care Wear's reach by the number of pattern requests she fills. Thanks to a generous donor, she now sends out a printed booklet containing more than seventy patterns for knitted, crocheted, and sewn hats, booties, kimonos, blankets, toys, and—sad but necessary—burial garments.

To date, she's sent patterns to about 15,000 volunteers.

"It's blossomed well beyond my expectations," Bonnie says of Care Wear, the gratitude and joy clear in her voice. She is quick to credit Hood College, whose motto is *Corde et Mente et Manu* (with Heart and Mind and Hand), for providing a supportive place, quite literally, for Care Wear to grow: her academic office. There, Bonnie responds to inquiries, sends out pattern booklets, keeps the paperwork necessary for Care Wear's nonprofit status, and writes a quarterly newsletter, a forty-plus-page collection of updates, articles, patterns, and notes from grateful hospital staff. She also maintains a database of more than 500 hospitals and March of Dimes chapters around the country, which can be accessed through Care Wear's website. The database provides detailed information on the places that will accept preemie knits. When Bonnie's position at Hood was reduced to half time a while back, her volunteer work with Care Wear quickly filled the remaining hours. "When I'm not working for Hood," she says, "I just move over to the other side of the room."

It's impossible to knit a preemie hat and not think about the preemie. First of all, you're struck by the very fact that a human can be so small—some weigh only ten or twelve ounces. Then you start to wonder how such a baby can stay alive. Then you think of the parents, and how anxious and sad those touch-and-go weeks are before the baby is allowed home—or not. Then you think of preemies you once knew, like the tiny boy you babysat in high school, who is now in high school himself, a basketball star.

"I think the appeal is that these are innocent victims," Bonnie says of her devotion to preemies. "Sometimes insufficient prenatal care is the cause, or poor nutrition, or alcohol, or smoking, or illness and infection." And sometimes it just happens—a baby is born too soon and no one knows why. Many of her volunteer knitters,

★ ★ ★ ★ ★ ★ ★ ★ ★ ★ ★

## KNITTING FOR BABIES NEAR YOU

• To learn the knitting needs of your local hospital, either find one near you on the Care Wear website or contact the hospital's director of volunteers, the director of child life, the nurse manager of the nursery or neonatal intensive care unit, or the director of pediatrics.

• Ask for guidelines on sizes and materials, as well as any other restrictions or particular needs.

• Bring or send a sample of your knitted item to the hospital liaison. Send a sample in each size you plan to make, and label the samples accordingly. After reviewing the samples, the hospital staff can decide which sizes or types of items will be most useful.

★ ★ ★ ★ ★ ★ ★ ★ ★ ★ ★

## MORE KNITTING-FOR-BABIES ORGANIZATIONS

**Newborns in Need**
www.newbornsinneed.org
Newborns in Need is a nonprofit charity based on Christian principles that sends clothing and bedding (handmade or purchased) and other baby supplies to sick and needy babies and their families.

**Stitches from the Heart**
www.stitchesfromtheheart.org
Stitches from the Heart is a charity organization and nonprofit store created to help premature babies all over the country. It provides opportunities to knit, crochet, or sew clothing and blankets for these babies.

★ ★ ★ ★ ★ ★ ★ ★ ★ ★ ★ ★ ★

she points out, have been in this situation themselves, or know someone who was, and this experience is powerful motivation. "You're expecting the Gerber baby," one hat recipient wrote to Bonnie, "and you get an infant that's two pounds, and you're not sure he's going to survive."

The care taken in the knitting reflects this concern. "The items I've seen are as beautiful as something you or I would make for our grandchildren," Bonnie says. "The workmanship is absolutely marvelous. The unique situation," she adds, "is that these donors will never see the recipients wearing the items; they're just hopeful that what they knit will be useful." To bolster volunteers, Bonnie requires that each hospital on her considerable list send an acknowledgment —if not a personal note—to the knitters who donate. And while NICU staff are understandably busy, most comply. "It was like Christmas when the box arrived!" is a common staff response, revealing yet another benefit of the

preemie hats. If they cheer the people involved in the hands-on efforts to keep these babies alive—people for whom a bad day at work is when someone dies—maybe the care they provide will be a little more tender, the tense NICU environment a little more peaceful.

In 2004, Bonnie was awarded the Knitter of the Year award by *Knitter's* magazine and Lion Brand Yarn Company in recognition of her efforts to further knitting and community service. While Bonnie was "tickled" to receive the award, it's clear her greatest rewards don't come in the form of ceremonies and prizes. On a filing cabinet near her desk, Bonnie has hung a photo of a strapping six-foot-two football player. Colleagues often mistake him for her son, but Bonnie doesn't have children of her own. "He's a Care Wear preemie," she corrects them, his photo sent in by a grateful mother who now knits for Care Wear herself. In the letter accompanying the photo, she noted, "I still have his hat." ★

# Care Wear Preemie Jester Hat

## —DESIGNED BY CATHY GILROY—

THESE ADORABLE LITTLE HATS NOT ONLY
WARM THE HEADS OF TINY INFANTS, BUT
HELP TO ENLIVEN AN OTHERWISE STERILE
NEONATAL WARD AND MAY EVEN BRING
SMILES TO THE FACES OF ANXIOUS
PARENTS. THE PATTERN IS WRITTEN FOR A
STANDARD PREEMIE-SIZE HAT. HOWEVER,
YOU CAN CREATE HATS TO FIT ALL SIZES OF
BABIES BY VARYING THE NEEDLE SIZE AND
YARN WEIGHT.

FINISHED MEASUREMENTS
10-12" circumference

YARN: Approximately 75 yards washable
sportweight yarn (preferably acrylic)

*Shown in Sirdar Snuggly DK (55%
acrylic/45% nylon) and GGH Maxima
(100% extra-fine superwash merino wool)*

NEEDLES: 1 set double-pointed needles
(dpn) size US 3 (3.25 mm)
1 set double-pointed needles (dpn) size
US 5 (3.75 mm)
*Change needle size if necessary to obtain
correct gauge.*

NOTIONS: Yarn needle

GAUGE: 24 sts and 30 rnds = 4" (10 cm)
in Stockinette stitch (St st) using larger
needles

## Brim
Using larger needles, CO 60 sts,
distribute sts evenly on three needles.
Join for working in the rnd, being careful
not to twist sts. Change to smaller
needles. Begin k1, p1 rib; work 20 rnds
even.

## Hat
Change to larger needles and St st (knit
every rnd); work 20 rnds even. Redistrib-
ute sts on two needles, placing 30 sts on
each. (Alternatively, you may BO all sts.)
Cut yarn, leaving an 18" tail.

## Finishing
Graft the hat opening shut using the
Kitchener st. If you bound off the hat
opening, close it using the Mattress st.

Make 2 pompoms (see page 126) and sew
them *very securely* to the points of the
hat. (Alternatively, sew ribbon bows,
ribbon roses, or other soft embellishments
to the points.) Using yarn needle, weave
in all ends. ★

# Caps for Kids

IT GOES WITHOUT SAYING THAT A PREREQUISITE FOR ANYONE STARTING A CHILDREN'S CHARITY IS A DEEP LOVE FOR KIDS. FOR BONNIE LAWLESS, WHO, WITH COFOUNDER NANCY LA FRAMBOISE, BEGAN CAPS FOR KIDS IN 1984, THIS IS ABSOLUTELY TRUE. "I'VE ALWAYS HAD A SOFT SPOT FOR CHILDREN," SAYS BONNIE, WHOSE PERSONAL LIFE IS PROOF: SHE HAS RAISED SIX KIDS OF HER OWN AND FOUR FOSTER CHILDREN, AND HAS WORKED WITH KIDS IN NEED IN QUEBEC AND VENEZUELA. ACTING ON THIS KIND OF DEVOTION OVER THE TWENTY-PLUS YEARS OF CAPS FOR KIDS' EXISTENCE, BONNIE, NANCY, AND YARN SHOP OWNERS ALL OVER THE COUNTRY HAVE COLLECTED WELL OVER A MILLION HATS FOR UNDER-PRIVILEGED CHILDREN, ALL HANDKNIT OR CROCHETED BY DOTING VOLUNTEERS. ☮ Like many knitting-for-peace movements, Caps for Kids seeks to keep the fruits of knitters' efforts local. "The focus was to distribute the caps in the area where they were made," Bonnie says, "because everybody's backyard has needy children." But instead of establishing a nationwide network of chapters, as many knitting charities have, Bonnie took advantage of a well-established network of which she was already a member—a network of knitting shop owners.

"Caps for Kids came out of a business problem I was having in my own yarn shops," Bonnie says, speaking of the Yarn Garden stores she once owned in Concord and Fremont, California. "People would buy an extra ball of yarn for their own insurance, and then bring it back one or two years later. You can't sell it because it's one ball, an odd lot. I had to figure out how to turn this into a positive. I kept asking myself: What can you do with one ball of yarn? All I kept coming back to was a cap—a cap for an underprivileged child."

Marketing her newly founded Caps for Kids as a way for customers to use up that last ball of yarn, Bonnie printed up flyers and began slipping them in bags along with her customers' merchandise. Her customers responded, and the caps began coming into the store. "We hung them on a clothesline strung across the ceiling of the Concord store until the whole ceiling was covered with caps," she recalls in a gentle, grandmotherly voice. "Then we began putting them in the other store as well." In those pre-Internet days, the flyers, the clothesline, and a little publicity were enough to launch Caps for

Kids nationally. "We began getting caps in the mail from people who had been traveling through and picked up a flyer," Bonnie says. After a mention in *McCall's Needlework* magazine flooded Bonnie's shop with calls about Caps for Kids, she decided to make it a nonprofit organization. From there, Bonnie says, using the exact words of so many knitting charity founders, "it took on a life of its own.

"In order for a charity like this to work," says Bonnie, "it has to be good for everybody. It has to be good for the stores who are doing

**KNITTING FOR CAPS FOR KIDS**
• For more information on Caps for Kids, or to find a yarn store collecting caps near you, visit www.craftyarncouncil.com/caps.html.

• You can also send completed caps directly to:

Caps for Kids
2500 Lowell Road
Ranlo, NC 28054

it, because it takes a lot of time. It has to be good for the people who are making these caps, and of course it's good for the recipients. So if it's a win-win-win situation, it's going to be successful."

Although Nancy and Bonnie have both retired in the years since its inception, Caps for Kids is still active under the umbrella of the Craft Yarn Council of America's Warm Up America! Foundation (see "Everybody a Warm Body," page 58). CYCA offers a collection point for hats not distributed through local yarn stores (Bonnie still collects them too), and keeps a database of yarn stores across the country that will accept them. The hats are given to children from infants to teenagers through nationwide nonprofit organizations like the Salvation Army and Toys for Tots as well as community churches, food pantries, women's shelters, and child advocate programs. They're largely distributed in the month of December, just in time for winter and the holidays.

A bit of Bonnie's heart goes out with every cap sent. "Children are really victims of their environment," she sighs. "That environment shapes their life, and if you can do anything to help them, you really have to. I was brought up with the value that you have to give back to the community," she continues. "What's one cap? Well, to one child, one cap might mean warmth, and that's important to me." ★

# Caps for Kids Swirled Ski Cap

THIS HAT FEATURES A UNIQUE CONSTRUCTION TECHNIQUE. THE BODY IS WORKED FLAT, FROM SIDE TO SIDE, WITH A VERTICAL STRIPE PATTERN. SIMULTANEOUSLY, DECREASES ARE WORKED ON ONE END AND INCREASES ON THE OTHER, WHICH GIVES THE WORK A PARALLELOGRAM SHAPE—A RECTANGLE WITH A SLANT. WHEN THE PARALLELOGRAM IS SEWN TOGETHER, THE STRIPES NATURALLY SWIRL AROUND THE HAT.

FINISHED MEASUREMENTS
Small (Medium/Large)
16 (18)" hat circumference

YARN: Approximately 130 yards worsted-weight yarn (MC)
Approximately 70 yards worsted-weight yarn (CC)

*Sample shown in Classic Elite Yarns Bazic Wool (100% superwash wool)*

NEEDLES: One pair straight needles size US 7 (4.5 mm) or one 16" circular (circ) needle size US 7 (4.5 mm)

One pair straight needles size US 8 (5 mm)
*Change needle size if necessary to obtain correct gauge.*

NOTIONS: Yarn needle

GAUGE: 16 sts and 24 rows = 4" (10 cm) in stripe pattern (unstretched)

## Hat
Using larger needles and MC, CO 30 (40) sts.
Row 1: Knit.
Row 2: P2tog, purl to last st, k1-f/b.
Row 3: Knit.
Row 4: Repeat Row 2.
Row 5: Knit.
Row 6: Repeat Row 2.
Change to CC.
Row 7: Purl.
Row 8: K2tog, knit to last st, k1-f/b.
Row 9: Purl.
Row 10: Repeat Row 8.
Row 11: Purl.
Row 12: Repeat Row 8.
Change to MC.
Row 13: Purl.

Repeat Rows 2-13 a total of 7 (9) times. BO all sts.

## Brim
Using smaller needles and MC, pick up and knit 1 st in every row along one side of the panel for the bottom of the hat—86 (108) sts. (Alternatively, you may sew the side seam of the hat at this point and work the brim in the rnd with a 16" circ needle.) Work 20 (30) rows/rnds in k1, p1. BO all sts knitwise.

## Finishing
If you knit the brim flat, sew the cast-on and bound-off edges together to create hat shape. Thread a length of yarn through the side without the brim, gathering the top of the hat together. Pull yarn tight, leaving a tail. Make pompom (see page 126) and sew it to the top of the hat, using remaining tail. Using yarn needle, weave in all loose ends. Turn up brim. ★

# Children in Common

LEGEND HAS IT THAT ON CHRIST-MAS EVE IN RUSSIA, WHEN CHIL-DREN ARE FAST ASLEEP, A KINDLY OLD WOMAN NAMED BABUSHKA ("GRANDMOTHER" IN RUSSIAN) WANDERS THE COUNTRYSIDE IN SEARCH OF THE CHRIST CHILD. SHE NEVER FINDS HIM, BUT AS SHE TRAVELS, SHE LEAVES TOYS AND TRINKETS FOR CHILDREN, GIFTS THEY DISCOVER UPON WAKING ON CHRISTMAS MORNING. ⊕

For children in orphanages across Eastern Europe and Russia, it's always Christmas when Karen Porter or one of her contingency arrives. Karen, of Baltimore, Maryland, is the founder and driving force behind Children in Common, a relief effort organized to bring supplies to children living in desperately poor orphanages. Like Babushka with her gift-laden basket, Karen arrives with suit-cases literally vacuum-packed with needful things: toiletries, medical supplies, school supplies, toys, and—best of all—thick, woolen socks, vests, and sweaters, all handknit by tireless and loving volunteers. In poorly heated institutions (indoor temperatures during the winter average 45°F), few things are needed more.

Karen is intimately aware of the needs of these children; her own sons, Anton and Alexander (Sasha), were the first children from Moscow to be adopted when the country opened its borders to American adoptions, and she's been told she was the first parent to travel to Russia to adopt. What she saw there changed her life.

"The conditions in the orphanages were terrible," she says as though she would never have believed it if she hadn't seen it with her own eyes. "My younger son came home literally in rags.

There was no heat, plaster was falling from the walls, the rugs were threadbare. I vowed I would do everything I could to help the kids who remained."

Life is bleak in a post-Soviet orphanage. The youngest children, in the "baby homes" (children are separated by age into different orphanages), usually spend most of their days sleeping, and parents who adopt babies often discover that their children suffer from sensory deprivation and attach-ment issues. Sadly, though, very few of the children in the orphan-ages *can* be adopted. The majority, whose parents are still alive and have not relinquished their rights, must stay. So, at age sixteen, after spending nearly all of their lives in an orphanage, these children are turned out into the community, where most find themselves poorly equipped to lead independent lives. With no money, job skills, and only a fifth-grade education, 80 percent of deinstitutionalized children turn to prostitution, drug addiction, or suicide. Fortunately, thanks to groups like Children in Common and the deeply devoted caregivers who work at the orphanages, there is hope for at least some of these orphans.

"The directors of the orphanages are ecstatic to get hand-made things," says Karen, who emphasizes that handknit items warm much more than body parts. "They feel that a person's energy is left in the item that they've made, so it makes it much more beneficial for a child to wear." For these children, warm socks and sweaters, blessed with a knitter's touch, hold an important place in their hierarchy of needs.

Children in Common fills two roles, both as a relief effort and a social network through which adoptive parents can share information and support. In addition to providing warm knitted clothes and other necessary supplies, it helps the orphanages set up programs in which older children can learn skills such as woodworking, sewing, and—fittingly—knitting, so they will be able to clothe themselves, find jobs, and barter for other needs once they leave.

Children in Common uses the slogan "OK, OK, OK!" to illustrate the ways knitting can benefit these orphans—boys and girls alike. The first OK refers to "orphan knitting": the precious sweaters and socks hand-knit by volunteers with orphans in mind. The second stands for "orphaned knitting," encouraging knitters to dig out and finish abandoned projects that—though probably long out of style—will still warm an orphan. Finally, there's "orphans knitting," where knitting is taught through life skills programs at many institutions. Children in Common supplies children in these orphanages with knitting needles, yarn, and instruction books in Russian or other appropriate languages.

> "
> **There is no trust more sacred than the one the world holds with children. There is no duty more important than ensuring that their rights are respected, that their welfare is protected, that their lives are free from fear and want and that they grow up in peace.**
> "
>
> KOFI ANNAN

Karen is a lifelong knitter—the rebel in a family of crocheters—so it was natural for her to see knitting as a solution to the problems in these orphanages. "These kids need something warm and cuddly," she says a little wistfully, as if she would gather them all in a soft blanket right now if she could. In preparation for a goodwill trip in 1998, during which she and others brought "massive suitcases of stuff" to fourteen orphanages in Russia, Karen got serious with the knitting component. "Before that trip, I managed, in eight months, to knit a *gross* of hats." She laughs in disbelief. Still, there were more kids to warm than she could possibly knit for. "I put a little call out to the Knitlist," she says, and the publicizing of Children in Common's knitting needs began and ended there.

The Knitlist, a giant community of online knitters, took up the cause immediately. The plea for help coincided with the forming of a new subgroup of the list,

Socknitters, that kicked off with a challenge to its members: Could two hundred pairs of children's socks be hand-knit in time for the next goodwill trip? "We got over *one thousand* pairs," Karen says, emphasizing every word. "It was amazing. And it's just grown and grown from there."

For some on the Socknitters list—and certainly for many who heard of Children in Common through other means—the plight of these orphans is keenly felt. Claudia Krisniski, the designer of the Children in Common socks on page 104, promotes sock-knitting for these children during community knitting nights in her yarn shop, Countrywool, and on the Internet. She says of her involvement with Children in Common, "I can't not do it. I have Lithuanian roots, and much of my extended family in Lithuania was wiped out in World War II. Some of the kids in the orphanages may be related to me." Adoptive parents, or other family members, are also generous with their time and skills.

"When they see the conditions in these orphanages, or when they see how much an adopted child has enriched their lives, they're happy to give," Karen says.

Karen likes to use Derrevannoe, an exceptionally shabby orphanage in Russia's far north, as an example of Children in Common's success. "The buildings were falling down around the kids," she recalls from her first visit there in 1998. "The floors were rotting; the wind was coming in around the windows. And those children were hard, with stonelike, angry features. When we went back"—after helping the director there establish woodworking and sewing programs, and after distributing suitcase after suitcase of socks, sweaters, and supplies—"they saw that we cared, that we did remember them, and that they mattered. Now, we've seen these kids grow up. Each time we go back, they remember us, and they're happy to see us. Seeing them blossom and be so proud of the things they've made and what they can accomplish proves that you can turn your life around, even with just a little bit of hope. You don't have to be given a lot—just the hope and the opportunity—to really change your life." ★

**KNITTING FOR CHILDREN IN COMMON**

• The most needed items in Eastern European orphanages are socks, sweaters, and vests to fit children ranging in age from six months to sixteen years. Outerwear items such as hats and mittens are also welcomed, but are less necessary for day-to-day living. For links to more Children in Common patterns, visit www.childrenin common.org.

• The yarn used for these items should contain as much wool or animal fiber (llama, alpaca, etc.) as possible—at least 80 percent—for maximum warmth.

• Children in Common also accepts knitting supplies such as yarn and needles (no larger than size 5, as knitters in these countries typically use smaller needles).

• Send completed items and donated supplies to:

Children in Common
c/o Adoptions Together
5750 Executive Drive, Suite 107
Baltimore, MD 21228
(410) 869-0620

# Children in Common Socks

—DESIGNED BY CLAUDIA KRISNISKI—

THESE SOCKS, BECAUSE OF THEIR SHORT LEG LENGTH AND LARGER GAUGE, ARE QUICKER TO KNIT THAN MOST SOCKS, AND A GOOD WAY TO PRACTICE SHORT-ROW SKILLS. THE CHILDREN IN RUSSIAN ORPHANAGES USE THEM MOSTLY AS SLIPPERS FOR INDOOR WEAR INSTEAD OF SHOES; HENCE THEIR SHORTER LEG. IF YOU WISH TO MAKE A MORE TRADITIONALLY SHAPED SOCK, SIMPLY KNIT THE LEG TO THE DESIRED LENGTH.

DEPENDING ON THE YARN YOU CHOOSE (REMEMBER THAT WOOL IS PREFERABLE FOR CHILDREN IN RUSSIA) THESE SOCKS WILL BE QUITE THICK WHEN FINISHED—AND THE HEAVIER AND STURDIER THEY ARE, THE BETTER. TOWARD THAT END, AN OPTION FOR A SLIGHTLY FELTED SOCK IS INCLUDED.

FINISHED MEASUREMENTS
To fit Small (Medium, Large, Extra-Large) Child 6½ (7¼, 8, 8¾)" circumference

YARN: 100 (125, 150, 200) yards worsted-weight yarn

*Sample socks shown in Peace Fleece Worsted Weight (70% wool/30% mohair) and Cascade Yarns Cascade 220 (100% wool)*

NEEDLES: One set of double-pointed needles (dpn) size US 5 (3.75 mm) *Change needle size if necessary to obtain correct gauge.*

NOTIONS: Yarn needle, stitch markers

GAUGE: 20 sts and 24 rnds = 4" (10 cm) in Stockinette stitch (St st), using light worsted-weight yarn
18 sts and 24 rnds = 4" (10 cm) in Stockinette stitch (St st), using medium to heavy worsted-weight yarn

## Cuff

CO 32 (36, 40, 44) sts. Distribute sts evenly on three needles. Join for working in the round, being careful not to twist sts: place marker (pm) for beginning of rnd. Work in k1, p1 ribbing until cuff measures 2" from the cast-on edge.

## Leg

Change to St st (knit every rnd), working even until the leg measures 4" from the cast-on edge, or to desired length, such as 4 (5, 6, 7)" for a more traditional sock. On last rnd, pm after st 16 (18, 20, 22).

## Heel Shaping

The Heel is worked back and forth using short rows. This technique utilizes short row wraps (SRW), worked as follows: Slip 1 st, bring working yarn to opposite side of work (front if knitting, back if purling), slip st back to left needle, bring working yarn back to original side of work.
Row 1 (RS): Knit 15 (17, 19, 21) sts (this is 1 st before side marker), SRW next st and turn work.
Row 2 (WS): Purl 14 (16, 18, 20) sts (this is 1 st before marker at beginning of rnd), SRW next st and turn work.
Row 3: Knit to 2 sts before side marker, SRW next st and turn work.
Row 4: Purl to 2 sts before beginning of rnd marker, SRW next st and turn work.
Continue as established, working 1 less st each row, ending on WS row with p8 (9, 10, 11), or to 4 sts before marker. Turn work.

## Turning Heel

With RS facing, knit 8 (9, 10, 11) sts, place new marker. Knit all the way around the sock, ending back at new marker. When working across Heel sts, knit wraps together with the wrapped sts (see page 127).

## Reverse Heel Shaping

SRW at next st, turn, and work as follows:
Row 1: Purl 8 (9, 10, 11) sts, SRW, turn.
Row 2: Knit 9 (10, 11, 12) sts, SRW, turn.
Row 3: Purl 10 (11, 12, 13) sts, SRW, turn.
Row 4: Knit 11 (12, 13, 14) sts, SRW, turn.
Continue until all Heel sts have been worked, ending with a WS row. Turn work. Work 1 rnd around entire sock as before, working wraps together with the wrapped sts. On either side of heel, in the gap between the heel and the foot, pick up 1 extra st, twist it, and knit it together with the following st to prevent a hole.

## Foot

Continue working in the rnd until foot measures 2-4 (5, 6, 7-8)" long (ranges are given to accommodate very small or large feet).

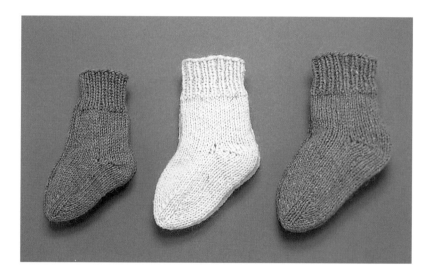

## Toe

Distribute sts evenly on two dpn.
Rnd 1: K1, k2tog, k to last 3 sts, ssk, k1. Repeat across second needle.
Rnd 2: Knit.
Repeat Rnds 1 and 2 until 8 sts remain. Cut yarn, leaving an 8" tail. Thread through remaining sts, draw tight, and fasten off securely, or graft sts together using the Kitchener stitch (see page 126). Using yarn needle, weave in all loose ends.

## Felted Version

To make an extra-thick felted sock, follow the above instructions, using size US 8 (5 mm) needles and adding ¾" to the length of the leg and ¾" to the length of the foot. When completed, machine-wash and machine-dry the socks. ★

# Orphans for Orphans Sweater

## —DESIGNED BY JEANNE DYKSTRA—

THIS COZY SWEATER IS MADE USING A NOVEL CONSTRUCTION TECHNIQUE THAT KEEPS THE KNITTING INTERESTING AND THE FINISHING MINIMAL. THE CENTER FRONT AND BACK ARE WORKED IN SIMPLE RECTANGULAR PANELS; STITCHES ARE PICKED UP FROM THOSE PANELS TO KNIT THE SIDES AND SLEEVES ALL THE WAY DOWN TO THE CUFF. WITH SIDE SEAMS KNIT OR GRAFTED TOGETHER, LITTLE SEWING IS REQUIRED AT THE END. LIKE MANY PROJECTS IN THIS BOOK, THIS ONE IS A BLANK SLATE ONTO WHICH YOU CAN APPLY YOUR FAVORITE STITCH PATTERNS AND COLOR COMBINATIONS. IT'S DESIGNED TO USE UP "ORPHAN" BALLS OF YARN IN YOUR STASH.

FINISHED MEASUREMENTS
23 (26, 29)" chest

YARN: 350 (475, 600) yards worsted-weight yarn

*Shown in Green Mountain Spinnery Mountain Mohair (70% wool/30% mohair)*

NEEDLES: One pair straight needles size US 8 (5 mm)

One 24" circular (circ) needle size US 8 (5 mm)
*Change needle size if necessary to obtain correct gauge.*

NOTIONS: Stitch holders, yarn needle, crochet hook size G/6 (4 mm), stitch markers (optional), cable needle (cn) (optional)

GAUGE: 16 sts and 24 rows = 4" (10 cm) in Stockinette stitch (St st)

NOTES: If choosing different stitch patterns for Front and Back Panels, take care to match gauge.

CABLE PATTERN: (CP) (optional)
(10 sts; 4-row repeat)
Rows 1 and 3: (WS) k2, p6, k2.
Row 2: (RS) P2, slip next 2 sts to cn, hold in front, k2, k2 from cn, k2, p2.
Row 4: P2, k2, slip next 2 sts to cn, hold in back, k2, k2 from cn, p2.
Repeat Rows 1–4.

## Front Panel

CO 20 (21, 22) sts. Begin in St st (or desired stitch or stripe pattern); work even until piece measures 9½ (11½ ,14)" from beginning. BO all sts loosely.

## Back Panel

CO 20 (21, 22) sts. Work as for Front Panel in St st (or desired stitch or stripe pattern); work even until piece measures 11½ (13½, 16)" from beginning. BO all sts loosely.

## Sides

Lay both panels in front of you with the Back on the left, the Front on the right, and the bound-off (neck) edges facing each other. With circ needle, and beginning at lower right corner of Front Panel, pick up and knit 36 (43, 52) sts along the side of the Front Panel. Using the Backward-Loop Cast-On (see page 126), CO 20 sts for neck opening. Beginning at upper left corner of Back Panel, pick up and knit 42 (51, 58) sts along the side of the Back Panel—98 (114, 130) sts total. After picking up side sts, turn work so WS is facing. *

PLAIN VERSION: Work in St st (or desired stitch or stripe pattern) for 3½ (4½ , 5)", ending with a WS row.

CABLED SLEEVE VERSION: Beginning at *, work the cable pattern as follows:
Rows 1 and 3 (WS): Purl 44 (52, 60) sts, place marker (pm), CP, pm, p44 (52, 60).
Row 2 (RS): Knit to marker, CP, knit to end.
Row 4: Knit to marker, CP, knit to end.

Work as established for 3½ (4½, 5)", ending with a WS row.

Knit 25 (31, 37) sts and place on holder. Work across center 48 (52, 56) sts in pattern as established, place remaining 25 (31, 37) sts on holder.

*Note: Sts on holders are joined later using Three-Needle BO or Kitchener st to form side seams. If you prefer to sew side seams, BO sts on holders on last RS row.*

## Sleeves

Working on center 48 (52, 56) sts, dec 1 st each side every 4th row 11 (12, 13) times. Continue in pattern until sleeve measures 7½ (9, 9½ )" from beginning, ending with a WS row—26 (28, 30) sts remain.

CUFF: Work 6 rows in garter stitch, ribbing, or any stitch pattern that prevents the edge from rolling. BO all sts loosely in pattern.

Make second side and sleeve to match the first.

## Finishing

Transfer side sts to needles and join side seams using Three-Needle BO (see page 127) or Kitchener st (see page 126). If you bound off sts earlier, join using Mattress st. Sew Sleeve seams.

## Neck Edge

Using crochet hook, work one row of single crochet around entire neck

opening. Work one row of Backward Crochet (see page 126) and fasten off.

## Lower Edge Band

Using circular needle, pick up and knit 1 st in each st around lower edge of garment. Work same st pattern as for sleeve cuff until Band measures 2" from pick up row. BO all sts loosely in pattern. ★

## Kids Knitting for Peace

Kids and knitting for peace go hand in hand. Not only is kids' knitting good for those in need, but it's also good for kids themselves, providing benefits that range beyond the physical to the cognitive and even social—what a way to harness kids' creativity and natural sensitivity for others. Many charity knitting projects are so simple—think of a rolled-brim hat or an afghan square—that they make perfect tools for teaching kids to knit.

Pat McLeavy-Payne, an elementary school teacher who leads a group of student knitters called Knits of the Round Table at the Galloway School in Atlanta, Georgia, teaches children to knit by getting them involved in Warm Up America! "I start them out on sixteen stitches in garter stitch," she says, "and they work their way up to thirty-five, enough for a square."

Warm Up America! founder Evie Rosen concurs. "When I had my shop," she remembers, "a group of my customers and I went into a couple of fourth-grade classrooms, and we taught the kids to knit. They produced an afghan or two, and some of them took to it immediately. The young boys were especially good at it. They approach it as an engineering project."

Michelle Kennedy, who teaches knitting at an after-school program at Jefferson/Coulee Montessori School in La Crosse, Wisconsin, uses squares in a different way. "My kids begin knitting small squares," she says. "When they're done, I make them think: What could this square become? What could it make that a kid might enjoy?" From this brainstorming, the squares become everything from bean-bags to pillows to pirate eye patches and are donated to kids at a local Salvation Army home, which provides emergency shelter for families in need.

Once a square can be knit, as Michelle's students have discovered, the sky's the limit. Kids can just as easily assemble blankets for Project Linus, Binky Patrol, afghans for Afghans, their local animal shelter, and more. "Project Linus has a particular motivation," says its president, Carol Babbitt, "because the blanket is going to another kid."

"When a child's in a hospital or shelter," adds Mary Balagna of Project Linus, "at first everybody rallies around them to support them, then they kind of end up on their own. The family's still there, but their friends move on. When they get a blanket made by another child, it's like they have new friends who care about them."

Knitting for peace not only gives kids a skill that will bring them enjoyment their entire lives, but teaches them valuable lessons about caring for others who might not be as lucky as they are. One of the appeals of Binky Patrol for its publicist, Carolyn Berndt, was that it was a charitable activity she could do with her daughter. "It's one of my goals," she says, "that when she becomes an adult, charitable work will be second nature to her."

To encourage a love of knitting and helping others among children, the Craft Yarn Council of America, through its Warm Up America! Foundation, places particular emphasis on teaching children to knit, especially in schools. The CYCA recently awarded a grant to the Helping Hands Foundation, a nonprofit mentoring program in Oregon that trains knitters and crocheters to teach their skills in after-school programs.

"There's already a mandate to do community service in many schools," says CYCA's Mary Colucci, "and now knitting is enjoying more media exposure, so the kids think it's cool—it's kind of the right time. Kids can start out by doing something good for others, and then they have a skill that lasts a lifetime." It also offers an opportunity to build bridges and form relationships between children and adults of all ages, particularly for a generation of children who may not have learned knitting from parents or grandparents. "I believe we are letting some very precious things die by not teaching our children these crafts," says Carol Babbitt. "I think children need to learn to sew, to knit—it encourages self-sufficiency."

Knitting offers personal benefits as well. It builds kids' self-esteem, encourages problem solving, improves math and motor skills, and calms and focuses them. Knitting for peace engages them in a creative, constructive activity that teaches them to work together toward a common goal. Best of all, it's an equal-opportunity craft: Any kid can make a difference, regardless of age, skill, family income level, or gender.

Evie Rosen illustrates this point. "Early on in Warm Up America!," she says, "a teacher in one of the New York schools was knitting during a study hall, and one of the football players asked her to teach him to knit. She didn't quite believe him the first time, but when he asked the second time, she taught him. Pretty soon the whole football team was knitting." She laughs. "I love that story."

**LEARN MORE**
For more information on teaching kids to knit and involving them in knitting-for-peace efforts like Warm Up America!, visit these websites:

www.craftyarncouncil.com/teach.html
www.warmupamerica.org/kids.html
www.lionbrand.com/BK4K Archive.html

# Mother Bear Project

THE BACK ROOM AT BOREALIS YARNS IN ST. PAUL, MINNESOTA, IS BUZZING THIS MORNING. AROUND A SMALL TABLE ARE GATHERED HALF A DOZEN WOMEN, MEMBERS OF A GROUP THAT MEETS THE THIRD WEDNESDAY OF EVERY MONTH TO KNIT. THEY ALL CHATTER AND LAUGH LIKE OLD FRIENDS, AND EVEN NEWCOMERS FEEL AT HOME BEFORE LONG. IT'S THE EASY CAMARADERIE THAT COMES WHEN PEOPLE GATHER WITH A COMMON INTEREST LIKE KNITTING; IT'S THE QUICK BONDING THAT RESULTS WHEN THE PURPOSE IS SHARED. THESE WOMEN, THOUGH ENGAGED IN SEPARATE TASKS, ARE UNITED IN THEIR PASSION: MAKING TEDDY BEARS FOR MOTHER BEAR PROJECT. ☮ Through this effort, handknit bears are sent to provide comfort and love to children in South Africa, specifically those who have been orphaned by or are themselves infected with HIV/AIDS.

"Look at this," announces Amy Berman, holding up a brown bear with a yellow and blue outfit. "This one came from Australia!" Amy, a tall, slender, forty-something mom, is the original Mother Bear. She founded the organization in 2003 after reading an article in *Marie Claire* about the plight of children in South Africa.

Barb Lundeen and her fourteen-year-old daughter Kristen are tracing and cutting small hearts out of red felt; one will be sewn to the chest of every bear donated to Mother Bear Project. Across the table, Mary Ellen Hennen is stitching those hearts on, a sewing kit at one side and a pile of bears at the other. Amy's mother, Gerre Hoffman, a woman with neat gray hair and reading glasses perched on her nose, is the bear doctor ("Our own Florence Nightingale," says Amy). It's her job to repair those bears—of the hundreds donated from knitters around the country and beyond—that might not have turned out quite as the knitter intended. Mostly, there are head and neck issues. "Cinching the neck is crucial," Gerre says, shaking her head over a particularly thick-necked bear. "It gives the body needed shape and dimension." She threads a running stitch above the bear's shoulders and gives it a tug. "There," she says, tilting her head and smiling at her patient. "That's all it took."

It's important to Amy and her knitters that the bears look as good as possible—as cuddly and friendly as they can be—for the South African children who will receive them. In many cases, these bears are all the children have. Casualties of the AIDS epidemic, many have lost their parents and, as a result, their homes; to date, more than 11 million South African children have been orphaned by AIDS. Many have AIDS themselves, and have contracted it in the horrifying way detailed in the *Marie Claire* article that inspired Mother Bear Project. "There's a myth in South Africa that you can make yourself immune from AIDS by having sex with a virgin," Amy explains, and this myth leads to the rape of thousands of infants and girls; the youngest mentioned in the article was two months old. South African child protection workers quoted in the article put out a call for toys to comfort these children—some so poor they use glass bottles as dolls—and Amy, deeply struck by the news of raped babies, took this to heart.

"I've always been concerned about the plight of women and children in the world," says Amy. "But I'm just a mom—I can't be pulling children out of brothels in India." Immediately upon reading the story, however, she knew what she would do. When her own

children, Anna and Zach, were born, Amy's mother knit them teddy bears using a pattern given to her by an English friend, a pattern with which English mothers had knit bears to comfort their own children during World War II, when many of them were sent away to safe places. Amy's children had loved those bears hard until they were threadbare, and Amy was convinced this was just what those South African children needed. "I wanted to send them something heartfelt, something that would be a labor of love," says Amy. "That's what these bears are." It was Zach who named the project when he dubbed Amy "mother bear."

Amy claims she's not a great knitter, and many of the friends she recruited to join her in her efforts had never knit at all, but the bear pattern is so simple, and the cause so contagious, that many joined her efforts quickly. "I told my mom, 'If we could send twenty-five bears; if we could help twenty-five kids,'" she says. "Then it

★ ★ ★ ★ ★ ★ ★ ★ ★ ★ ★ ★

One woman who hands out bears in South Africa told Amy these stories: During a terrible rainy season, a family headed by a young girl had to evacuate their home. Her younger brother insisted on going back for his bear, saying, "It has a heart on it and means somebody loves me." They rescued the bear, and minutes after they left the house, it was washed away by the rains. Another small girl in Zambia, ostracized at her school for having AIDS, told her teacher her bear was her only friend. It was buried with her when she died.

★ ★ ★ ★ ★ ★ ★ ★ ★ ★ ★ ★

was one hundred." She laughs. "Eighty-three hundred bears later," she gestures around the room. "Here we are."

Now, Amy receives about 400 bears a month, all of which she collects in her home, packs by hand in boxes of fifty, and ships to South Africa. Originally, Amy shipped the bears directly to the South African child protection unit mentioned in the *Marie Claire* article, but as word has spread of Mother Bear Project, other contacts have been made. A Minnesota group sending school supplies to Zambia caught wind of the project and offered to send bears as well. Schools and orphanages in Africa put in requests regularly; in some areas, bears are handed out to orphans on the streets. Amy sends shipments of bears twice weekly, asking knitters to contribute $3 with each bear to help cover the staggering costs of shipping and duty fees. To date, Amy reports that all bears have reached their destinations safely.

Back at Borealis, people are stopping by on their way to someplace else, too busy to knit but wanting to pick up brochures or drop off a new batch of bears. "I constantly have them attached to me," says one knitter who drops by. "I'm a bear evangelist."

While word of mouth is the most common method of publicizing Mother Bear Project locally, the project's captivating website has drummed up responses from knitters nationwide. Even yarn companies like Muench Yarns and Alchemy Yarns have become contributors, donating yarn that local volunteers wind into balls (it takes three in different colors to make a bear) and distribute.

Other local groups have taken up the cause as well. The Minnesota Knitters' Guild adopted Mother Bear Project as one of its charity knitting efforts. Nuns of the School Sisters of Notre Dame in Mankato knit bears and treasure the handwritten, fingerprint-smudged notes they receive in return. And at St. Therese Care

Center, an assisted living home in Hopkins, resident knitters, including a ninety-seven-year-old woman, churn out about twenty bears a month. Amy tallies every bear sent by every knitter, wherever they may be, and those tenacious knitters who contribute one hundred bears are honored with membership in the "Hundred-Bear Club." Members receive a pin, handcrafted by and purchased directly from artisans in South Africa, featuring a red heart with "100" on it.

In the face of a pandemic, there doesn't seem to be much that knitters—or a small stuffed bear—can do. But you'd be surprised. "You can't underestimate what the bears mean to the children who receive them," says Amy, who traveled to Zambia in 2004 and saw the children's situations firsthand. "I saw so much sadness there—all these children orphaned, literally sleeping on the streets. Everyone I met took in AIDS orphans," she says, "but there are just too many." At the time of her visit, about 65,000 children were living on the streets in Zambia, and 350 people were being buried a day. To a small child enduring this, a soft, cuddly bear with a red heart means a great deal.

The bears bring blessings to the knitters as well as the children who receive them. Amy tells of a female inmate who crocheted a bear in prison, stuffing it with shoulder pads because that was the only stuffing she had. She tells of knitters in hospice care who knit bears up to the very end. Each bear contributed contains a bit of the unique knitter who made it. There are bears wearing glasses, braids, ponchos, soccer uniforms, ballet outfits, and tennis shoes— bears who reflect a bit of the knitter's life in some way. "Everyone who contributes," Amy emphasizes, "is Mother Bear." In that spirit, each bear sent to South Africa arrives with a tag tied to its wrist, which reads, "With love, Mother Bear," and is signed by the knitter.

The knitting is winding down at Borealis; the hearts are being put away, and finishing touches are made on bears before they're set aside for the next box destined for South Africa.

"Oh dear, another neckless one," sighs Gerre, picking up a small white bear shaped like a star. She smiles down at it. "But he's got a sweet face."

"We'll give him a proportionately smaller heart," says Mary Ellen.

"No," says Gerre firmly. "He's a small bear with a big heart." ★

---

### KNITTING FOR MOTHER BEAR PROJECT

• Use only washable worsted-weight yarn for knitting the bears. Acrylic, cotton, and washable wools or wool blends are acceptable. Stuff them with polyester fiber fill, which is also washable.

• Do not attach buttons, beads, or any object that could be a choking hazard.

• Do not send store-bought bears or bears made from other patterns.

• When sending your knitted bear(s), include $3 per bear to help defray shipping costs to South Africa.

• Additional copies of the bear pattern are available from Mother Bear Project for $3 (again, the money goes toward shipping costs). With the pattern, Mother Bear Project will send arm tags for you to sign and attach to your bear, so the child receiving it will know which "Mother Bear" created it. If you send in a bear without an arm tag, volunteers at Mother Bear Project will sign your name to a tag and attach it.

• Red felt hearts will be sewn onto your bear(s) by volunteers at Mother Bear Project once they are received.

• For additional guidelines and answers to frequently asked questions, visit www.motherbear-project.org, or e-mail amy@mother bearproject.org.

• Send completed bears to:

Mother Bear Project
P.O. Box 62188
Minneapolis, MN 55426

# Mother Bear Project Teddy Bear

THIS BEAR IS WORKED IN ONE LONG PIECE, BEGINNING WITH THE FRONT LEGS AND TROUSER, FRONT SWEATER, FRONT AND BACK HEAD, BACK SWEATER, AND BACK TROUSER AND LEGS. ARMS ARE PICKED UP AND KNIT AFTERWARD. ONCE YOU GET THE BASIC PATTERN DOWN, YOU CAN EMBELLISH AND PERSONALIZE THE BEAR ANY WAY YOU WISH.

FINISHED MEASUREMENTS
Approximately 14" tall (size will vary with yarn and stitch patterns used)

YARN: Approximately 50 yards in each of 3 colors of washable worsted-weight yarn: MC (main color, for hands, feet, and face of bear), TC (trouser color), and SC (sweater color). Additional scraps of contrasting colors (CC) for scarf.

*Samples shown in Mission Falls 1824 Wool (100% superwash merino), Reynolds Signature (80% acrylic/20% wool), and Brown Sheep Company Lamb's Pride SuperWash (100% superwash wool)*

NEEDLES: One pair straight needles size US 7 (4.5 mm)

NOTIONS: Yarn needle, small amount of lightweight yarn or embroidery floss for face, polyester fiberfill

GAUGE: Gauge is not crucial for this project

## Leg and Trouser
Using MC, CO 10 sts; begin Garter st (knit every row); work 10 rows.
Change to TC and St st; work 20 rows, ending with a WS row; place sts on holder. (Alternatively, for a different look, you may continue working the bear in Garter st.)
Work second Leg and Trouser as above. Using TC, work 10 sts, then work 10 sts from holder—20 sts. Continue in St st; work 16 rows to finish trouser.

## Sweater
Change to SC; work 20 rows in St st (or the stitch pattern of your choice—seed stitch, cables, or stripes, for example).

## Head and Back
Change to MC, work in either St st or Garter st for 5½". (Stockinette stitch makes a smooth surface for embroidering the face; Garter stitch creates a furry-looking face.)

Change to SC, reverse the steps (sweater, trousers, and legs) to complete the back of the bear.

## Skirt Option
To create a "girl" bear with a skirt, hold the completed bear with the feet facing away from you and, RS facing, using TC, pick up and knit 28 sts evenly across the last row of the sweater front.
Row 1: Purl.
Row 2: *K1, increase 1 stitch, repeat from * across—42 sts.
Row 3: Purl.
Work even in St st for 14 more rows or to desired length.

## Hem
Change to CC.
Row 1: Knit.
Row 2: Knit (will form ridge on right side of hem).
Row 3: Purl.
Repeat Rows 2–3 until 3 ridges have been made.
BO knitwise on a purl row. This will make the hem curl under.

Add the skirt to the Back in the same manner.

## Scarf

Using SC or CC, CO 60 sts.
Work 3 rows in Garter st; BO all sts.

## Forming Head and Adding Arms

Fold bear in half along the middle of the head section, right sides facing out. Stitch together sides of head using Mattress st or whipstitch.

Open bear body out flat again. With RS facing, using SC, pick up and knit 16 sts (8 sts along the sweater front and 8 sts along the sweater back on either side of head) to begin arm.

Work 16 rows in sweater pattern.

Change to MC and Garter st; work 10 rows. BO all sts. Repeat for second arm.

## Assembling Bear

*Note: When stuffing, fill the bear but do not overstuff, or the bear will be stiff and the stuffing visible.*

HEAD: Fill head using small pieces of fiberfill to avoid lumps and provide a smooth base for embroidering the face.

ARMS AND BODY: Beginning at the end of each arm (bear's hands), sew sleeves and sweater body seams. Fill hands firmly. Stuff arms and body.

LEGS: Continue sewing lower body and legs, leaving an opening in the trouser crotch for stuffing. Stuff legs, making sure to fill feet. Sew trouser opening. If you chose the skirt option, sew skirt together at sides.

SHAPE NECK: Using MC, thread yarn through the last row of sts forming head. Draw yarn tight to shape neck, secure yarn and fasten off.

## Face, Scarf, and Tag

Embroider a face with yarn or embroidery floss. This will give your bear a "personality."
Sew diagonally across top corners of head and "pinch" ears for a rounded look. Tie scarf around neck and anchor securely to back of neck.

Write your first name on the tag; attach it to your completed bear's wrist with yarn. (Tags can be obtained from the Mother

Bear Project (see page 113), or a volunteer will sign your name to a tag and attach it once you've sent in your bear.) A red felt heart will be sewn on the chest before shipping. ★

# Knit

## —FOR—

# Peace

# Getting Started

While dozens of knitting-for-peace opportunities have been presented in this book, hundreds more exist. They range from highly organized movements with an international reach to regional knitting guilds and the group that gathers in your own church basement or local yarn store. You'll find many of these, along with scores of free charity knitting patterns, on the Internet. Others can be located by inquiring at local yarn stores, knitting guilds, and other places where people gather to knit. And if none is available to you, you may wish to start a knitting-for-peace group of your own.

## SURFING FOR PEACE
By typing "charity knitting" into your favorite Internet search engine, you'll discover more ways to knit for others than you could accomplish in a lifetime. Browse through your search results, and you're almost certain to find a cause that calls to you. Be sure to visit the website of the charity of your choice before you begin knitting to receive the most current information on needs and guidelines. The following websites offer particularly good lists of charity knitting opportunities:

### LION BRAND YARN
### CHARITY CONNECTION
**www.lionbrand.com/charity connection.html**
This page on the Lion Brand Yarn site allows knitters to search for charities by area of interest as well as by location. It also allows knitters to post their own charity knitting organizations, resulting in a wide selection of groups large and small, national as well as local. It's also an excellent source of free charity knitting patterns, many supplied by the organizations themselves.

### INTERWEAVE PRESS
### KNITTING FOR A BETTER WORLD
**www.interweave.com/knit/charities.asp**
Assembled by the editors of *Interweave Knits* magazine, this list arranges charities alphabetically and offers a description and contact information for each, as well as web links to most of the organizations.

### WOOL WORKS RESOURCES
**www.woolworks.org/charity.html**
Organized by state, this list is particularly helpful in locating knitting opportunities close to you. It offers a collection of free charity knitting patterns as well.

> 66
>
> # Peace-making is a healing process and it begins with me, but it does not end there.
>
> 99
>
> **GENE KNUDSEN HOFFMAN,**
> Quaker peace activist

BELLAONLINE CHARITIES
**www.bellaonline.com/subjects/ 206.asp**
This list goes beyond knitting to include other crafting for charities. It has a good list of opportunities in Canada too.

GROUP KNITTING FOR PEACE
There's power in numbers. Think of how your efforts will multiply when you make charity knitting a group endeavor. To get started, here are some ideas for enlisting others for knitting-for-peace projects.

• Start small. Begin by gathering a few like-minded, dedicated friends, then expand by publicizing your group in places knitters are most likely to look—yarn stores, coffee shops, or community bulletin boards.

• Pick an available central location for your meetings and reserve it on a regular basis. Consider members' homes, yarn stores, library community rooms, coffee shops, or meeting rooms in your place of worship.

• Choose a convenient time and date, and decide how frequently you'd like to meet—once a month, twice a month, once a week.

• Pick a charity your group is interested in supporting. Or pick several, focusing on one every month or every quarter. Alternatively, identify a need in your own neighborhood that could be filled by knitting.

• Supply extra yarn, needles, and instructions for basic charity knitting projects, and encourage others in your group to donate extra yarn in their stashes to your cause. (Be sure to verify the yarn requirements of your chosen charity first.)

• Easy charity knitting projects, like scarves and hats, are a wonderful tool for teaching others to knit. Invite interested nonknitters to your group, and be ready to teach (visit www.learntoknit.com, the Craft Yarn Council of America's website, for help).

## KNITTING FOR PEACE NEAR YOU

While there are many opportunities to knit for others across the country and overseas, some of the greatest needs that can be filled by knitting exist just down the street. In the shelter downtown, in the transitional housing program a few blocks away, even in the elementary school in your district,

people near you are in need of warm knit things. Here's how to find them, and how to knit for them.

• Consider what group of people you might be interested in serving with your knitting. Premature babies, children, elderly people, homeless families, people with AIDS, and teenage mothers can all benefit from knit things.

• Do some research to find places that accept knit items in your area. Depending on where your interest lies, check the phone book or do an Internet search for hospitals, nursing homes, or animal shelters in your area. Local branches of organizations such as the Salvation Army, the Red Cross, or the YMCA are also familiar with needs in your area and can suggest places to donate to. Or, utilize your community

network. Friends involved in volunteer activities, leaders at your place of worship, and schoolteachers are keenly aware of community members in need.

• Contact the director of the facility you're interested in supporting, and verify whether they would welcome knit items and which items, in particular, are most needed. Ask for guidelines on sizes and materials, as well as any other restrictions. Identify the best way to deliver the goods (many shelters, especially, have confidentiality requirements) and plan your knitting drives around times of the year when your efforts are most needed.

# Basic Mittens

THESE MITTENS ARE KNIT FIRMLY TO MAKE THEM WARM AND HARD-WEARING.

FINISHED MEASURMENTS
To fit Child Small (Child Medium, Child Large, Adult Medium, Adult Large) 5½ (6, 7, 8, 9)" in circumference

YARN: Approximately 75 (100, 125, 150, 175) yards worsted-weight yarn

*Samples shown in Reynolds Lite Lopi (100% wool) and Mission Falls 1824 Wool (100% superwash merino)*

NEEDLES: One set double-pointed needles (dpn) size US 7 (4.5 mm)
*Change needle size if necessary to obtain correct gauge.*

NOTIONS: Yarn needle, stitch markers, stitch holder or waste yarn

GAUGE: 18 sts and 24 rows = 4" (10 cm) in Stockinette stitch (St st)

## Cuff
CO 24 (28, 32, 36, 40) sts, distribute sts evenly on three needles. Join for working in the rnd, being careful not to twist sts; place marker (pm) for beginning of rnd. Begin k2, p2 rib; work even until Cuff measures 2½ (2½, 2¾, 3, 3)" from beginning.

## Thumb Gusset
Rnd 1: K12 (14, 16, 18, 20), pm, M1-L (see page 125), pm, k12 (14, 16, 18, 20) sts—25 (29, 33, 37, 41) sts.
Shape Thumb Gusset as follows:
Rnd 2: (increase rnd): K12 (14, 16, 18, 20), slip marker (sm), M1-L, knit st(s) between markers, M1-R (see page 125), sm, k12 (14, 16, 18, 20)—27 (31, 35, 39, 43) sts.
Rnds 3–4: Knit even.
Repeat Rnds 2–4 3 (3, 4, 5, 6) times, until there are 9 (9, 11, 13, 15) sts between markers—33 (37, 43, 49, 55) sts. Continue to end of rnd.

## Hand
Next Rnd: Remove markers as needed, k12 (14, 16, 18, 20), work 9 (9, 11, 13, 15) sts and place sts on waste yarn, k12 (14, 16, 18, 20) sts—24 (28, 32, 36, 40) sts remain for hand.

Continue even in St st until piece measures 5½ (6, 7½, 8, 9)" from the beginning.

## Top Shaping
Continuing in St st, Shape Top as follows:
Next Rnd: *K4 (5, 6, 7, 8), k2tog; repeat from * around—20 (24, 28, 32, 36) sts remain.
Knit 3 (3, 4, 4, 4) rnds even.
Next Rnd: *K3 (4, 5, 6, 7), k2tog; repeat from * around—16 (20, 24, 28, 32) sts remain.
Knit 2 (2, 3, 3, 3) rnds even.
Next Rnd: *K2 (3, 4, 5, 6), k2tog; repeat from * around—12 (16, 20, 24, 28) sts remain.
Knit 1 (1, 2, 2, 2) rnd(s) even.
Next Rnd: *K1 (2, 3, 4, 5), k2tog; repeat from * around—8 (12, 16, 20, 24) sts remain.
CHILD'S SMALL ONLY: Cut yarn, leaving a 6" tail, thread through remaining sts, pull tight, and fasten off securely. Using yarn needle, weave in all loose ends.
CHILD'S MEDIUM ONLY: *K1, k2tog; repeat from * around—8 sts remain. Cut yarn, leaving a 6" tail, thread through remaining sts, pull tight, and fasten off

securely. Using yarn needle, weave in all loose ends.

CHILD'S LARGE ONLY: *K2, k2tog; repeat from * around—12 sts remain.

Next Rnd: *K1, k2tog; repeat from * around—8 sts remain. Cut yarn, leaving a 6" tail, thread through remaining sts, pull tight, and fasten off securely. Using yarn needle, weave in all loose ends.

ADULT MEDIUM AND LARGE ONLY:

Knit 1 rnd even.

Next Rnd: *K3 (4), k2tog; repeat from * around—16 (20) sts remain.

Knit 1 rnd even.

Next Rnd: K2, k2tog; repeat from * around—12 (15) sts remain.

Next Rnd: K1, k2tog; repeat from * around—8 (10) sts remain. Cut yarn leaving a 6" tail; thread through remaining sts, pull tight, and fasten off securely. Using yarn needle, weave in all loose ends.

## Thumb

Place sts from waste yarn on dpn. Join for working in the rnd, picking up 1 st in the gap where join occurs, and pm for beginning of rnd—10 (10, 12, 14, 16) sts. Work even in St st until Thumb measures

¾ (1¼, 2¼, 3¼, 3¾)" from beginning of Gusset.

Next Rnd: *K1, k2tog; repeat from * around, ending k1 (k1, k2tog, k2, k1)—7 (7, 8, 10, 11) sts remain. Cut yarn leaving a 6" tail. Thread through remaining sts, pull tight, and fasten off securely. Using yarn needle, weave in all loose ends. Make second mitten to match.

## Finishing

Block mittens, shaping them as desired. If desired, embroider an embellishment with contrasting yarn. ★

# Basic Rolled-Brim Hat

## —DESIGNED BY JOANNE TURCOTTE—

EVERY CHARITY KNITTER NEEDS A PATTERN FOR A BASIC, ROLLED-BRIM HAT. ITS USES ARE UNLIMITED: KNIT IT OUT OF WOOL FOR AN AFGHAN CHILD, USE A WARM AND WASHABLE BLEND FOR A CHILD AT A LOCAL SHELTER, OR FIND VERY SOFT, LUXURIOUS FIBER FOR A FRIEND—OR STRANGER—UNDERGOING CHEMOTHERAPY.

A BASIC HAT PATTERN LIKE THIS IS ALSO A BLANK CANVAS FOR YOU TO PLAY WITH COLOR, EMBELLISHMENT, AND STITCH PATTERNS, EXPANDING YOUR KNITTING REPERTOIRE AND USING UP ODDS AND ENDS OF YARN. EXPERIMENT WITH STRIPES, FAIR ISLE PATTERNS, TOPKNOTS, AND POMPOMS— ANYTHING YOU THINK THE RECIPIENT MIGHT LIKE.

FINISHED MEASUREMENTS
To fit Child (Adult Small, Adult Large) 16 (18, 20)" in circumference

YARN: Approximately 100-150 yards worsted-weight yarn

*Samples shown in Brown Sheep Lamb's Pride Worsted (85% wool/15% mohair) and GGH Maxima (100% merino wool)*

NEEDLES: One set of double-pointed needles size US 7 (4.5 mm)
One 16" circular (circ) needle size US 7 (4.5mm), optional
*Change needle size if necessary to obtain correct gauge.*

NOTIONS: Stitch markers, yarn needle

GAUGE: 20 sts and 24 rnds = 4" (10 cm) in Stockinette st (St st)

## Hat

Loosely CO 80 (90, 100) sts. Distribute sts evenly on three needles or use circ needle. Join for working in the rnd, being careful not to twist sts; place marker (pm) for beginning of rnd.

Begin Stockinette st (knit every rnd); work even until piece measures 6 (6½, 7)" from beginning.

## Shape Crown

*Note: If using circular needle, change to dpn when necessary for number of sts remaining.*
Begin decreasing as follows:
Rnd 1: *K8, k2tog, repeat from * around— 72 (81, 90) sts remain.
Rnd 2 and all even rnds: Knit.

Rnd 3: *K 7, k2tog, repeat from * around— 64 (72, 80) sts remain.
Rnd 5: *K 6, k2tog, repeat from * around— 56 (63, 70) sts remain.
Rnd 7: *K 5, k2tog, repeat from * around— 48 (54, 60) sts remain.
Rnd 9: *K 4, k2tog, repeat from * around— 40 (45, 50) sts remain.
Rnd 11: *K 3, k2tog, repeat from * around— 32 (36, 40) sts remain.
Rnd 13: *K 2, k2tog, repeat from * around— 24 (27, 30) sts remain.
Rnd 15: *K 1, k2tog, repeat from * around— 16 (18, 20) sts remain.
Rnd 17: *K2tog, repeat from * around— 8 (9, 10) sts remain.

## Optional Topknot

Continue knitting 2 sts together until 4 sts remain. Using 2 dpns, work I-Cord (see page 126) until Cord measures 2" from beginning.

## Finishing

Cut the yarn, leaving a 12" tail. Thread through remaining sts, then draw up tight, and fasten off securely. Using yarn needle, weave in all loose ends. Tie I-Cord in a knot. ★

# Abbreviations

**BO:** Bind off

**CC:** Contrast color

**Circ:** Circular

**Cn:** Cable needle

**CO:** Cast on

**Dpn:** Double-pointed needle(s)

**K:** Knit

**K2tog:** Knit 2 sts together.

**K1-f/b:** Knit into front loop and back loop of same st to increase 1 st.

**MC:** Main color

**M1 or M1-L (make 1-left slanting):** With tip of left-hand needle inserted from front to back, lift strand between 2 needles onto left-hand needle; knit strand through back loop to increase 1 st.

**M1-R (make 1-right slanting):** With tip of left-hand needle inserted from back to front, lift strand between 2 needles onto left-hand needle; knit it through front loop to increase 1 st.

**P:** Purl

**Pm:** Place marker

**Rnd:** Round

**RS:** Right side

**Sc (single crochet):** Insert hook into next st and draw up a loop (2 loops on hook), yarn over and draw through both loops on hook.

**Skp (slip one stitch, knit one stitch, pass slip st over knit stitch):** Slip 1 st knitwise, then knit next st. Insert left needle into front of slipped st. Pass slipped st over knit st and off right needle.

**Sl (slip):** Slip stitch(es) as if to purl, unless otherwise specified.

**Sl st (crochet slip stitch):** Insert hook in st, yarn over hook, and draw through loop on hook.

**Sm:** Slip marker

**Ssk (slip, slip, knit):** Slip next 2 sts to right-hand needle one at a time as if to knit; return them back to left-hand needle one at a time in their new orientation; knit them together through back loop(s).

**St(s):** Stitch(es)

**St st:** Stockinette Stitch

**Tog:** Together

**WS:** Wrong side

**Yo:** Yarn over

# Special Techniques

**Backward Crochet:** *Working from left to right,* insert hook into next stitch, yarn over and draw up a loop; yarn over and draw it through both loops on hook.

**Backward-Loop CO:** With working yarn, make a loop (using slipknot) and place on right-hand needle [first st CO], *wind yarn around thumb clockwise, insert right-hand needle into front of loop on thumb, remove thumb and tighten stitch on needle; repeat from * for remaining stitches to be CO, or for casting on at end of a row in progress.

**Garter Stitch:** Knit every row when working straight; knit 1 round, purl 1 round when working circular.

**I-Cord:** Using a double-pointed needle, cast on or pick up required number of sts; working yarn will be at left-hand side of the needle. * Transfer needle with sts to your left hand, bring yarn around behind work to right-hand side; using a second double-pointed needle, knit sts from right to left, pulling yarn from left to right for the first st; do not turn. Slide sts to opposite end of needle; repeat from * until cord is desired length. *Note: After a few rows, the tubular shape will become apparent.*

**Kitchener Stitch:** Using blunt yarn needle, thread a length of yarn approximately 4 times the length of section to be joined. Hold pieces to be joined wrong sides together, with the needles holding the stitches parallel, both ends pointing in same direction. Working from right to left, *insert yarn needle in first stitch on front needle as if to knit, pull yarn through, remove st from needle; insert yarn needle into next st on front needle as if to purl, pull yarn through, leave st on needle; insert yarn needle into first st on back needle as if to purl, pull yarn through, remove st from needle; insert yarn needle into next st on back needle as if to knit, pull yarn through, leave st on needle. Repeat from *, working 3 or 4 stitches at a time, then go back and adjust tension to match the pieces being joined. When 1 st remains on each needle, cut yarn and pass through last 2 sts to fasten off.

**Pompom:** Use a pompom maker or the following method: Cut 2 cardboard circles to diameter of pompom desired. Cut 1" diameter hole in center of each circle. Cut small wedge out of each circle to allow for wrapping yarn. Hold circles together with openings aligned. Wrap yarn tightly around circles. Carefully cut yarn around outer edge of circles. Wrap 12" length of yarn around strands between circles and tie tightly. Slip circles off completed pompom; trim pompom but leave end of tie untrimmed and use to attach pompom to project.

**Ribbing:** Although rib stitch patterns use different numbers of stitches, all are worked in same way, whether straight (in rows) or in the round. Instructions will specify how many sts to knit or purl; the example below uses k1, p1.

Row/Rnd 1: * K1, p1; repeat from * across, (end k1 if an odd number of stitches).

Row/Rnd 2: Knit the knit stitches and purl the purl stitches as they face you.

Repeat Row/Rnd 2 for rib st.

**Short Row Shaping:** Work number of sts specified in instructions, wrap (SRW) and turn as follows: Bring yarn to front (purl position), slip next st purlwise to right-hand needle, bring yarn to back of work, return slipped st on right-hand needle to left-hand needle; turn, ready to work next row, leaving remaining sts unworked. When Short Rows are completed, or when working progressively longer Short Rows, work the wrap together with wrapped st as you come to it as follows: If st is to be worked as a knit st, insert right-hand needle into wrap, from beneath wrap up, then into wrapped st; k2tog; if st to be worked is a purl st, insert needle into wrapped st, then down into wrap; p2tog. (Wrap may be lifted onto left-hand needle, then worked together with wrapped st if this is easier.)

**Single Crochet (sc):** Insert hook into next st and draw up a loop (2 loops on hook), yarn over, and draw through both loops on hook

**Slip Stitch (crochet) (sl st):** Insert hook in next st (or st specified), yarn over hook, and draw through loop on hook.

**Stockinette Stitch (St st):** Knit on RS rows, purl on WS rows when working straight; knit every round when working circular.

**Three-Needle BO:** Place stitches to be joined onto two same-size needles; hold pieces to be joined with right sides facing each other and needles parallel, both pointing in same direction (to the right). Holding both needles in left hand, using working yarn and a third needle same size or one size larger, insert third needle into first stitch on front needle, then into first st on back needle; knit these 2 sts together; * knit next stitch from each needle together (2 stitches on right-hand needle); pass first stitch over second stitch to BO 1 stitch. Repeat from * until 1 stitch remains on third needle; cut yarn and fasten off.

# Acknowledgments

WHEN I BEGAN THIS BOOK, I EMBARKED ON A JOURNEY OF SORTS THAT WOULD TAKE ME AROUND THE COUNTRY AND EVEN THE WORLD (THOUGH PHYSICALLY, I RARELY VENTURED MUCH BEYOND MY DESK AND MY FAVORITE COFFEE SHOP). BUT AS WITH MOST JOURNEYS THAT SEEM TO BEGIN WITH ONE TRAVELER AND ONE IDEA, I FOUND MYSELF SELDOM ALONE. I'D LIKE TO THANK THOSE WHO HELPED PREPARE ME, THOSE WHO TRAVELED WITH ME, AND THE FASCINATING PEOPLE I MET ALONG THE WAY.

First and most important, I wish to sincerely thank all the contributors to this book—the designers, the founders of knitting charities, and the coordinators of self-help knitting organizations who offered their stories, their patterns, and their passion to *Knitting for Peace*. I have so enjoyed meeting and speaking with each and every one of you. Without you—and the thousands of charity knitters who eagerly support your organizations and so many others—this book would never be. I am deeply in awe at the transformation a handful of highly moved and motivated people can bring about in this world and for so many people. Each one of you has strengthened my faith in humanity. You are beacons of hope and true messengers of peace.

I've had the good fortune of working with my editor, Melanie Falick, for several years, and I wholeheartedly thank her for giving me this opportunity and so many others. Editor Christine Gardner further honed this manuscript, and Wendy Preston ensured that patterns were correct and clearly written. Scott Edelstein, a longtime friend and colleague, was an early cheerleader of this project and offered valuable insight from his perspective as a literary agent. Kiriko Shirobayashi, with her photographer's eye, and Diane Shaw and Kathryn Hammill of goodesign made this book beautiful. Many thanks also to photographer and friend Greta Ingvalson, who took my author photo in exchange for a pair of handknit mittens.

Thanks also go to the yarn companies that generously provided yarn for the samples knitted for this book. You have contributed in more ways than one, as all the samples knit for this book will be donated to the charities they represent.

I absolutely could not have written this book without the help and camaraderie of my knitting friends in the La Crosse, Wisconsin, area: Cathy Acker, Cam Buenzli, Michelle Kennedy, Laura Miles, Susan Omans, Susan Peterson, Eileen Przytarski, Jane Radloff, Chris Swain, Suzanne Toce, Mary

Veldey, and Peg Zappen, all true knitters for peace. They not only made or contributed to many of the projects photographed in this book, but, more priceless, they gave me their support, laughter, and countless evenings of knitting therapy. Thanks especially to Linda Sherony, a generous knitter whose yarn shop, Follow Your Heart, is the center of our universe. New York knitters Marisa Bulzone, Alexis Mentor, Kim Tyner, and Christine Gardner pitched in to fill last-minute knitting needs. And I offer a warm embrace to my friends Melody Moore and Kate Kjorlien, who not only knit for the book, but, as a writer and an editor, respectively, gave me so much encouragement and reminded me—through all the deadlines, bouts of writer's anxiety, and other crises—that I was making a dream come true.

With this book, I am also honoring the memory of Oleeta Hermanson, who taught me to knit nearly thirty years ago. Neither she nor I knew, in those afternoons spent in her living room, what an impact her lessons would have on my life. My parents, Jim and Selma Christiansen, have raised my sisters and me with great love, have taught us to work hard, and do not hide their admiration for us. Most deeply, I thank my husband, Andrew Miles, for believing in me more than I believed in myself. He is my North Star.

And finally, let me sing the praises of knitters for peace everywhere, who meet in yarn stores, coffee shops, church basements, and homes to knit for others they may never meet. We are interconnected, inextricably, in a powerful web of love and yarn.

> "
> **Peace is the only battle worth waging.**
> "
>
> **ALBERT CAMUS**

# Index